More P
Everyday Coaching

"*Everyday Coaching* challenges leaders to create coaching cultures, and then the authors present a map to do exactly that. The stories, conversations, and tools Virginia Bianco-Mathis and Lisa Nabors share will help leaders everywhere begin a pay-it-forward journey with unlimited results!"

—Marshall Goldsmith
Author of the Number 1 *New York Times* Bestseller, *Triggers*

"*Everyday Coaching* is an inspiring must-read for any executive who wants to increase his or her bottom line: a practical guide for establishing the highly touted coaching culture in your company. Filled with clear, step-by-step, no-nonsense instructions to bring a coaching mindset to an organization, *Everyday Coaching* also explains why a coaching culture will enable significant benefits. Business coaches will love this book, because it offers a proven recipe for successfully implementing a coaching culture."

—Kathy Harman, MCC, CSM
Author, *PRISM Teams*

"Virginia Bianco-Mathis and Lisa Nabors are two of the top coaching gurus in the world, and *Everyday Coaching* captures their wisdom and experiences in a remarkably clear and practical way. I highly recommend this book for anyone who wishes to effectively coach and lead others."

—Dr. Michael Marquardt
Founder and Past President
World Institute for Action Learning

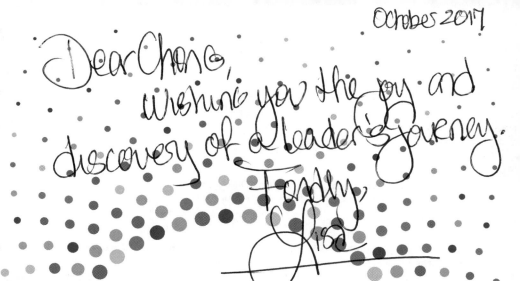

Dear Cherie,
Wishing you the joy and
discovery of a Leader Journey.
Fondly,
Lisa
October 2017

USING CONVERSATION TO
STRENGTHEN YOUR CULTURE

Everyday
Coaching

VIRGINIA BIANCO-MATHIS
AND LISA NABORS

PRESS

The Phillips case study in chapter 7 was reviewed and approved for publication by Alan Phillips.

ATD Press is an internationally renowned source of insightful and practical information on talent development, workplace learning, and professional development.

ATD Press
1640 King Street
Alexandria, VA 22314 USA

Ordering information: Books published by ATD Press can be purchased by visiting ATD's website at www.td.org/books or by calling 800.628.2783 or 703.683.8100.

Library of Congress Control Number: 2017942320

ISBN-10: 1-56286-993-0
ISBN-13: 978-1-56286-993-9
e-ISBN: 978-1-56286-687-7

ATD Press Editorial Staff
Director: Kristine Luecker
Manager: Melissa Jones
Community of Practice Manager, Human Capital: Ann Parker
Developmental Editor: Jack Harlow
Senior Associate Editor: Caroline Coppel
Cover Design: Derek Thornton, Faceout Studio
Text Design: Francelyn Fernandez
Printed by United Graphics, Mattoon, IL

Contents

Preface

In 2002, we introduced a coaching model for leaders that encouraged them to look at themselves and the ways in which they interacted with their teams and organizations. We suggested that they had a tremendous opportunity to leverage language in support of creating dynamic, results-oriented, and fun workplaces. In 2008, we looked at the bigger picture and shared our thinking as to how organizations could create coaching programs in support of relationships and results. We continued to emphasize that language is the driver of learning and development. We showed how dialogue can create strong teams with members who consistently deliver high-quality results and have fun while they do so. In 2017, we took the next logical step and expanded our thinking to include everyone within organizations.

Many authors and practitioners—Patrick Lencioni, Andy Andrews, Tom Rath, Marshall Goldsmith, Peter Senge, Laura Whitworth, Kim Scott, Brené Brown—have highlighted the human need to be seen and the power that is unleashed when that need is met. The content of this book will help you in your efforts to "see" yourself and others. In so doing, you will create an organization that is fueled by caring, direct communication between individuals who are committed to achieving extraordinary results.

In this book, we work from the premise that each person within an organization can learn a new language—dialogue—and use it to create a coaching culture characterized by excellence and continuous learning. Every person can bring their best ideas forward and collaborate with colleagues to coach, question, brainstorm, problem solve, and find solutions in a high-energy, solution-focused way. They can coach and be coached. We are excited to endorse the idea that everyone can learn something new; everyone can improve their skills; everyone can help their colleagues, customers, and stakeholders; and everyone can show up, every day, knowing that what they say and do can make a difference. We invite you to read this book, apply the content, and make a difference.

Acknowledgments

We have the best desktop publisher on the planet and we worship her. We have an equally stellar graphic artist whom we would be lost without. The team at ATD are a gift and we appreciate everything they do. We are blessed to live and work with people who are loving, smart, funny, curious, driven, and imperfect. We learn something every day from these individuals, our families, our clients, our students, our colleagues, our friends, and the many folks we meet during the course of our daily lives. We look forward to seeing everyone, every day, and we are grateful for the opportunity to do so. Finally, we acknowledge each other. After 30 years, we are embedded in each other's hearts and minds in a way that enables us to be more together than the sum of our parts. We "see" each other and we value what we "see." We know how lucky we are.

Virginia Bianco-Mathis
Lisa Nabors
August 2017

Introduction

Three years ago, we had completed a pilot of a special coaching program with Seyfarth Shaw LLP, a major international law firm. We were collating the measurement data and found ourselves marveling at the incredible results. The ripple effect of the program went well beyond our expectations and those of the client. So why was it so successful?

We created an internal cadre of coaches beginning with a one-day coaching boot camp. These coaches were top partners in the firm who took a day away from their many clients and court cases to learn basic coaching skills. Armed with job aids, guidelines, sample scenarios (both written and video), and an expert coach to call on every month, each attorney took on two coachees for eight months. The following year, the program was geographically expanded and eight more coaches were trained. The third year, eight more coaches were trained, and we planned to add an additional format—team coaching—to the program in the future. By the third year, some of the coachees had become coaches, and the coaching mindset had spread throughout the firm.

How did we get the attention of high-level law firm partners? The legal profession is going through a transition. Law firms are struggling to address the beliefs of younger generations, including Millennials, and engagement is becoming a serious issue. Young attorneys are taking positions at law firms, staying long enough to make money to pay off their student loans, and then leaving for other legal-related jobs in government, associations, and universities. Based on our experience working with law firms, the traditional law firm culture—uneven work-life balance, structured approaches, limited collegiality—is no longer viable in today's world. The managing partners of forward-thinking law firms are tackling this issue head-on.

So, how does a law firm create a more fluid atmosphere of engagement, provide more conversation and personal attention, identify long-term professionals earlier in their careers, give more personalized feedback, and help make associates feel appreciated and valued? And, in doing so, how do they increase the bottom line?

The coaching program we've described accomplished all this and more. The measurement data surfaced the following results: younger attorneys began bringing in clients earlier, the branding and public image of the firm became better because of an increase in publications, associates shared that they felt acknowledged and heard, and partners began giving more frequent and balanced feedback. Most important, everyone involved said they found themselves using the coaching skills in other parts of their lives, including how they interacted with clients. In one case, a client asked to only work with a "coaching" attorney because "the way he interacts with us is very energizing."

What was responsible for this turnaround? The coaching solution essentially became the catalyst for a major organization development effort. The culture changed. The language and tools of coaching—dialogue, powerful questions, advocacy, inquiry, global listening, personal accountability, action plans, and outcome tracking—became common place in the hallways and behind closed doors. Confronting sensitive issues, recognizing the reasoning behind opinions and actions, and reaching higher levels of understanding helped in solving problems and attaining higher levels of performance. With junior attorneys becoming more productive and engaged, the entire firm experienced growth and leadership at every level. The hidden potential of the firm was released.

Once we saw the success at Seyfarth Shaw, we asked, "How can we help other organizations gain this advantage?" We began to duplicate and enhance this approach within other organizations. The results were equally positive. And from there, this book began to take shape.

Building a Coaching Culture

Our 2008 book, *Organizational Coaching,* continues to serve an important purpose as a handbook for learning and practicing more structured coaching within organizations. With our success with Seyfarth Shaw and the emphasis on a total systems approach toward coaching, we began to see that anyone in an organization could become a coach. When more and more people within an organization learn coaching skills, the culture of the entire organization begins to change, which positively affects daily behaviors and conversations, problem solving, strategic thinking, personal growth, action planning toward defined measures, and mutual support. The concept of people giving one another meaningful and actionable feedback becomes the norm and not something that only occurs during annual performance appraisals. Furthermore, sharing insights to improve performance becomes acceptable and expected at all levels—up, down, and across. All employees have permission to ask questions to further learning.

Why is this permission given and even expected? Because everyone has been trained to do so with integrity and a special set of skills that makes dialogue powerful. With appropriate training and role modeling, leaders, managers, and co-workers take on the tenets of coaching:

- They believe that everyone is talented and can perform at a higher level.
- They believe that it is their job to help themselves and others unlock potential.
- They focus on solutions and actions.
- They deliver honest feedback even when the message might be difficult to hear, and they do it with appropriate dialogue skills and care.
- They focus on each interaction and their listeners.
- They listen for what is being said and not said.
- They stay in the moment.
- They hold a vision of possibility for themselves and others.
- They support others in achieving visions and desired outcomes.

Think of the possibilities when everyone in an organization is working and interacting with this mindset. In his first edition of *Masterful Coaching*, executive coach and thought leader Robert Hargrove (1995, 16) defined coaching as, "Challenging and supporting people in achieving higher levels of performance while allowing them to bring out the best in themselves and those around them." Additionally, colleagues and managers have all been trained to use conversation tools for transparent and supportive interactions. As a result, trust emerges. Employees, co-workers, bosses, and leaders begin to treat one another with respect and honesty, and not as objects. The continued practice of these skills begins to shape attitudes and behaviors and within two years, a culture can be transformed.

So how do you sustain this culture over time? As we learned from our work with Seyfarth Shaw, the organization must hardwire the new behaviors by instituting support structures. This can include:

- adding group coaching
- encouraging peer coaching
- assigning a coach to every new employee for six months
- assigning a coach to every newly promoted employee (no matter the level)
- offering coaching refresher courses (in person and online) to sustain the culture of coaching
- providing periodic coaching examples from YouTube with real employees
- volunteering to share coachees' successes
- offering coaching objectives with every performance evaluation
- instituting coaching into every management and leadership learning activity.

The implementation of coaching infrastructures is further addressed in chapter 8.

Coaching is part of mainstream corporate culture across the globe. While coaching was at one time associated with fixing toxic behavior at the top, the most frequently cited reasons to engage a coach are now developing high potentials, facilitating transitions, acting as a sounding board, and addressing derailing behavior (Coutu and Kauffman 2009). As coaching continues to evolve, it is useful to note that leading-edge organizations are strategically moving toward the development of coaching cultures. If we consider that "culture is the way we think, feel and act in relation to our workplace," a coaching culture is one where coaching is "the predominant style of managing and working together" (Sherpa Coaching 2017).

The International Coach Federation's *2016 Global Coaching Study* notes that "the use of coaching skills and approaches has expanded beyond professionally trained coach practitioners to include managers, leaders, and human resources and talent development professionals who apply these competencies in their daily workplace interactions" (ICF 2016, 3). This study also reports that coaching within organizations continues to increase every year and with it the credibility of coaching programs.

Coaching is recognized as a proven and accepted method for improving both tangible and intangible performance practices (Table I-1). Because of this, organizations are getting smarter in considering "the whole person" when measuring coaching results, and they are considering individual behavioral-based improvement, impact beyond the individual receiving coaching, and business results. This includes formulas and data on return on investment (ROI), financial impact, and impact on business metrics.

Lastly, this trend toward an organization-wide coaching culture is further emphasized by another finding from Sherpa Coaching. Namely, when participants were asked, "Why use coaching in your organization?" the answers went beyond individual and team impact to include major organization development efforts such as change management, growth, and productivity (2016, 32). Thus, in more innovative organizations, coaching is no longer being viewed as isolated one-on-one interactions between two people or with a team, but as broader within the context of being able to make a difference throughout the enterprise. You may determine the extent to which coaching affects the following positive results, as has been already proven in the research literature.

Table I-1. Measurable Coaching Results

Behavioral Results	Business Results
» More timely, direct communication » Quicker, more complete decisions » Increased employee engagement » More flexibility » Greater resilience » Stronger intra- and inter-departmental collaboration » More effective meetings » Decreased conflict » Less duplicative work	» Increased profits » Increased employee retention » Strengthened customer relationships » Sales and productivity goals and targets met or exceeded » Increased presence with customers » Shortened time to market » New hires onboarded more effectively » Learning transfer more quickly achieved » Organization adapts more quickly to change

Underlying Theory and Approach

As behavioral practitioners, we support a cognitive coaching approach. Namely, the coach becomes a thought partner with the coachee. Coaches— whether a boss, employee, colleague, or professional practitioner—help coachees identify limits in their thinking and aid them in adopting more accurate, useful reasoning and thinking patterns. This in turn leads to better relationships with others, improved decision making, and higher levels of performance (Stober and Grant 2006). The basis of cognitive coaching is the notion of "mental models." A mental model is a belief you may have about the world that causes you to act and behave in certain ways.

For example, you may believe that yelling is the best way to get your staff to perform well. This mental model might have come from your experience with past bosses or your own need for control. A technique that your boss, professional coach, or even an employee might use to give you feedback is something we call "the continuum of beliefs"—a picture of how your mental model influences your behavior and results (Table I-2). By discussing your existing and possible new beliefs, behaviors, and results, you might more clearly recognize how your existing thought pattern is causing the very result you are trying to avoid! With this insight, you can gradually entertain different mindsets and behaviors that can lead to more productive results.

Coaching someone from an old to new behavior doesn't happen overnight. Yet, with everyone using coaching approaches, the likelihood of adopting more successful behaviors increases substantially. This cognitive tool, and others covered in this book, represents the kind of theoretical underpinning that supports our organizational model. Such cognitive tools help you create a strong coaching base and produce evidence-based results.

The Purpose of This Book

Everyday Coaching is meant to be read by anyone who works in an organization and wants to learn and adopt a new way of working, talking, interacting, and succeeding. The premise is that the practice of using dialogue and tools in organizational coaching should be accessible to everyone—not just professional coaches—and that such accessibility and on-the-job behavior can transform an entire organization. Even if the rest of your organization doesn't adopt this premise, you can have a positive impact on your own performance and interactions with those around you.

Table I-2. Beliefs, Behaviors, and Results

Old Belief	Old Behavior	Old Result
I must yell to get people to do what I want.	I yell at my staff.	Staff members avoid me. They don't think things through and just do what I say. They don't respond in team meetings. I don't get what I want; quarterly goals are not met.
New Belief	**New Behavior**	**New Result**
People want to participate, and I can create more buy-in by listening to and including team members.	I hold open team meetings. I demonstrate that I'm listening by acknowledging feedback and incorporating the ideas of others into the plan. I practice dialogue, don't yell, invite others into the conversation, and form a partnership with others in getting the work done.	Staff are energized. Conversations are lively and participative. Staff take ownership for the results. They approach me with ideas and support. Quarterly goals are met.

Adapted and used with permission from Bianco-Mathis, Nabors, and Roman (2002, 112)

Coaching should happen up, down, and across. Specifically, you can practice coaching as a leader, manager, colleague, or professional coach by:
- managing or coordinating: as a supervisor, leader, or team lead [coaching down]
- contributing: as a staff person, employee, or team member [coaching up]
- collaborating: as a colleague, peer, consultant, or professional coach [coaching across].

Not every person can become a professional coach. There are specific requirements and credentialing for that role (see www.coachfederation.org for examples and more information). However, anyone can learn coaching language and can use those skills in daily interactions. As we will explain later, coaching can happen under many different circumstances:
- a normal coach and coachee relationship for six months
- a sales manager conducting monthly coaching visits with her salespeople

- a colleague coaching a team member on a new system; two team members walking down the hall and exploring how to form a better working relationship
- an employee approaching a boss and advocating for more ongoing feedback
- a director coaching his team on using a more consultative approach with internal customers.

This book introduces the Seven Cs Coaching Map, a series of seven steps you can learn and follow when approaching coaching situations. Although the map is addressed linearly, it often unfolds iteratively. Each chapter provides practical examples to help you utilize the rhythm and nuances of coaching dialogue. Coaching tool job aids are shared throughout, and you can download a graphic of the map at http://strategicperformance.net/downloads/7c.

Part 1, "Connecting Through Coaching," discusses the concept of changing our conversations (chapter 1) and utilizing the tools of dialogue: global listening, powerful questioning, and supportive advocacy (chapter 2). This part provides the foundation on which coaching organizations can be built.

Part 2, "Navigating the Seven Cs," includes four chapters covering the coaching map:

1. "Capture Context and Clarify Purpose"
2. "Collect and Feed Back Data"
3. "Create Options and Construct a Plan"
4. "Commit to Action and Celebrate Success."

Finally, Part 3, "Building a Coaching Culture," discusses how to empower an entire organization, retool the organizational DNA, and then create, implement, and align systems toward a new way of thinking and achieving high performance.

At the end of each chapter is a section called "Making It Real." Here, you will be asked to reflect on key chapter concepts and develop an action-oriented goal you can apply on the job. These exercises will help you hardwire your brain and integrate new information creatively and mindfully.

Our goal is to help you reframe how you look at organizations and your role as a champion of coaching language, the unleashing of potential, and the excitement of more positive working environments and results.

PART 1:
Connecting Through Coaching

Part 1 contains the underlying philosophy of this book. It highlights the importance of language and intention in managing coaching conversations, whether it's a structured coaching session with a professional coach or a fluid conversation in the hallway between colleagues. Also introduced are the Seven Cs Coaching Map and the powerful language of dialogue—the essence of fostering shared meanings and goal achievement for individuals and entire organizations.

1

Changing the Conversation

Changing the language you use with others can build relationships, strengthen communication, increase the speed of work, and create higher-quality results. The right conversations contribute to curiosity, learning, and action. Consider the following coaching examples and note how they illustrate the seven Cs.

Imagine you are a director within an IT company and you decided several months ago to work with a coach. You and your team work very well together, but you realized you would like to improve in the areas of delegation and making feedback stick. Because your company allows directors and senior leaders to obtain an outside coach from a pool of pre-identified resources, you interviewed two possible coaches based on a connection you felt after reviewing their resumes and background.

You ultimately chose Charles. You have had a great six-month coaching experience with him. First, you and Charles established ground rules and agreements on measurable goals, action plans, homework assignments, tools, field practice, length and frequency of meetings, confidentiality, and expectations. You knew you had chosen the right coach because you felt comfortable and safe.

Charles made it clear that he was there to help you discover and leverage the beliefs, actions, and results that would lead you to success (Capture Context). Charles asked you insightful questions to get to the core of what you wanted to achieve and what that would look like six to eight months out (Clarify Purpose). To gain further input, you and Charles agreed that he would interview your six direct reports to obtain feedback on your leadership approach. Charles collated these data and presented you with four themes to consider and reflect upon (Collect and Feed Back Data).

You and Charles studied each theme and considered a range of possible ideas and actions that could help you achieve your objectives (Create Options). This led to the creation of an action plan, complete with desired end results and field assignments that you would pursue over the next several months (Construct a Plan). Every two weeks, you and Charles discussed the results of your practice, zeroed in on further behavioral tips, focused on how to stay on track, and created ways to reach your goal—inviting others in your department to support you and asking other executives to share their winning strategies (Commit to Action).

Although there were several challenges involving excessive travel and one very difficult employee, you began to integrate and practice your new skills and tools. Over time, you and others could see that your way of making sure employees were engaged in their work and moving toward accountable results led to an entire shift in increased performance. There was a part of you that would have liked the process to have happened in half the time, but you realized it was necessary to exert consistent effort and commitment over time to choose and make new skills a part of your daily repertoire (Celebrate Success).

If you look at Table 1-1, you can see that we moved through the entire Seven Cs Coaching Map. You might consider the example with Charles a successful coaching situation.

Table 1-1. Seven Cs Coaching Map

Step	Actions and Tools
Capture Context Capture the details and parameters of the situation by asking questions that surface the problems or opportunities to be explored.	» Assess the situation: use powerful questions and global listening. » Determine the best approach and ascertain roles, readiness, and commitment. » Establish ground rules, rules of engagement, expectations, and process. » Surface problem or opportunity areas to explore.
Clarify Purpose Clarify the specific goal(s) and objective(s) that the coachee wants to achieve.	» Pinpoint the results the coachee wishes to achieve. » Determine performance versus potential. » Determine the existing situation compared with desired results.

Step	Actions and Tools
Collect and Feed Back Data Consider data gathered through a variety of methods to further inform purpose and potential.	» Gather data through methods that fit the situation: performance appraisals, observation, and surveys. » Sort data into themes. » Add themes to purpose and objectives to enrich pathways and insights. » Discuss perception versus reality and the consequences of doing nothing. » Be straight "with care."
Create Options Create possible options for achieving the goals.	» Brainstorm options. » Discuss pros and cons of different pathways. » Zero in on the most productive option(s) to pursue. » Discuss chosen option(s) in terms of future steps, reality testing, challenges, and skills or knowledge.
Construct a Plan Construct an action plan with objectives, desired results, steps, benchmarks, and field assignments.	» Construct an action plan with clear next steps. » Consider benchmarks, homework tasks, practice assignments, and measures of movement.
Commit to Action Commit to specific actions to practice and try in between each coaching meeting or until each desired goal is achieved.	» Refer to and update action plan in between and at each coaching meeting. » Choose actions to pursue for the next meeting. » Determine present beliefs, behavior, and results in contrast to future beliefs, behaviors, and results. » Develop winning strategies. » Manage ego, impatience, fear, and other barriers.
Celebrate Success Celebrate each step forward, mapping progress, breakthroughs, improvement, and interim and final results.	» Track and assess progress with an action plan and other behavior tools. » Enroll others to observe and give feedback. » Employ regular self-assessments. » Note minor and major steps toward desired goals. » Reflect on and reinforce developed skills and behaviors supporting desired results. » Turn new behaviors and results into daily activities. » Practice "self-coaching."

But this coaching map can be applied to everyday workplace interactions, too. Let's consider a second example.

You're walking to a meeting with Gail, one of your co-workers in the marketing department. You admire Gail's experience with statistical analysis of marketing data. While walking, Gail expresses her concern over a second presentation she's scheduled to give to the executive group on her recent market analysis. She thinks the first presentation went well, but notes that the executives didn't seem excited to take the actions she was recommending.

You ask Gail a few questions to zero in on what she thinks went well and where she believes she could have done better (Capture Context). You ask, "Pretend that your next presentation is fabulous. Share with me why it is fabulous—what are you doing and what are the results?" (Clarify Purpose). With a bit more conversation (Collect and Feed Back Data), you help Gail narrow down the areas she wants to "nail" and what she wants to happen because of her presentation. You support Gail and encourage her to think of ways she can work on her presentation to achieve her stated goals (Create Options). She decides to sit down with her co-worker Mark and ask for feedback because he was at her first presentation. She also decides to observe Jose, another co-worker, the next day when he gives his presentation to the board and to also ask Nancy, an executive known for her great presentations, to help her with messaging and delivery (Construct a Plan and Commit to Action).

Gail thanks you for your thoughts. You share with her that you found it helpful to get Nancy's help last year and that you are sure she will find Nancy's input worthwhile. Then you say, "You know, because Mark will also be at your second presentation, I wonder if you can ask him to help you during the meeting in some way. Can you think of some ways he might do that?" After more conversation, Gail believes it would be wise to have Mark take notes during her presentation so she can make sure she's able to put her ideas into practice. You share with Gail that you think this is a well-thought-out plan and that she will likely be successful in getting the senior team to implement her recommended actions (Celebrate Success).

What happened in the second scenario? Clearly, this was not a formal coaching experience. It was more casual, fluid, and flexible. You and Gail are colleagues and the entire coaching conversation happened while walking to a meeting. We might call this "coaching in the moment." Yet, as you can see, the same seven coaching steps shown in Table 1-1 were utilized just as in the formal coaching session. Furthermore, you were able to support Gail and offer options without telling her what to do. You created a safe environment for Gail that enabled her to delineate her goal, discover what had to be done, and gave her the confidence to move beyond her fears.

These two examples encapsulate what this book is about: using dialogue and coaching tools in either a structured or informal way to change conversations and support action.

Coaching Environments and Conversations

When we say we want everyone within organizations to conduct coaching conversations, we are not advocating the dilution of professional coaching. Rather, we are supporting the notion of taking the best of what professional coaching has to offer—the dialogue, tools, and mindset—and leveraging it to enhance organizational performance through meaningful conversations.

This is not an easy task. We all have developed different perspectives and styles of talking. We have learned there are certain rewards and punishments for saying or not saying certain things. Whether it is because it might not be politically correct or because we feel unsure how to express ourselves, we keep many of our thoughts to ourselves—even the good ones. Consequently, we often don't learn how to share feelings and thoughts productively. We come to organizations speaking "nondialogue," or as one of the fathers of dialogue, Chris Argyris (1977), explains it, "We revert to defensive routines."

In other words, rather than talk productively, we talk as to not cause any discomfort. This is fascinating because we live in language. What gets done or not done, expressed or not expressed, understood or not understood, is all because of language. As you will see, coaching conversations require dialogue, and learning dialogue is like learning a new language.

This is further explored in chapter 2. For now, it is useful to acknowledge that our differences in language span geography, syntax, personality, social norms, education, community, gender, upbringing, and DNA passed down over centuries. Fortunately, despite these differences, organizations can make choices about the kind of environments they wish to foster. And a major element of focusing environmental culture is how people talk to one another. People can talk at one another (discussion), or they can ask about and share the reasoning behind their words (true dialogue). Dialogue creates a shared pool of meaning that leads to greater understanding, problem solving, and decision making. As Daniel Goleman (1998) so eloquently says in his book on emotional intelligence, real conversations are the internal conversations in our heads. The reflect what we actually think and feel.

With basic conversation, real thoughts and feelings stay hidden. Consider the following exchange:

> **Paul:** John, what's going on with the Johnson contract? We have a lot on the line with that one.
>
> **John:** It's driving me crazy. He keeps changing his mind from meeting to meeting.
>
> **Paul:** Oh, come on. You have dealt with clients like that before. Work it out and make sure you stay within budget.
>
> **John:** Yep. That's what I'm trying to do.

How do you think John feels after this exchange? To what extent was Paul helpful? How much more prepared is John to handle this client? Chances are, John does not feel very supported and now has the added pressure of "staying within budget." The lack of information sharing and problem solving here is two-sided. How much did Paul learn about what is going on with the client? To what extent does he know what John has tried and what the issues are other than that the client keeps changing his mind? How would you rate Paul's support of John in this exchange? Paul's only support of John seems to be limited to a reference to, "You have dealt with clients like that before." If John and Paul were using true dialogue, they would be sharing their thoughts and feelings. They would be setting the stage for collaborating and learning. Consider this exchange:

> **Paul:** John, you look frustrated or annoyed, I can't tell which. Are you having problems with the project team?
>
> **John:** Is it that noticeable? I guess it is written all over my face. I'm both frustrated and annoyed! Yes, the project team is having difficulties and the real problem is the client.
>
> **Paul:** How is the client being difficult and how is that affecting the contract? What's going on?
>
> **John:** Johnson keeps changing his mind. I have had clients change their minds and I know how to manage such situations and keep the client happy. What's making this difficult is Johnson keeps blaming me and

the team. I've tried using change reports and showing him that everything we are doing is in line with what he shared in the last meeting. Unfortunately, he comes up with all these "far out" ideas in between the meetings, and I'm having trouble managing that behavior.

Paul: Interesting. You say he doesn't respond positively to change reports or being reminded of what he said before? Can you think of a way to move him forward, not making a big deal about him changing his mind, while keeping everything within the scope of the project?

John: That's my point. That's what I keep trying to do. I'm stuck.

Paul: Remember about two years ago—I know it was a while back—you were assisting me with Jane Morgan. She was a real pain, remember?

John: I sure do. I can't believe how you kept your cool from meeting to meeting. Let me see. I remember you stayed positive. You always complimented her on her great ideas. Oh, wow, I remember now; you kept saying, "Oh, I see you have done some additional thinking from the last time we talked."

Paul: That's right. I never demonstrated any frustration. In fact, remember that one time when she did a complete 180 and I said, "Wow, what creative thinking!" I saw you trying to hold in your laughter.

John: Yep. And, I get your point. She loved the compliments.

Paul: And, quite frankly, her additional ideas and thinking had merit from time to time. So, it was important for me to listen and figure out how her newest idea could either be easily done or whether it required an additional adjustment to the contract.

John: Yes, I see what you mean.

Paul: A question I like to ask myself is, "How can I build a bridge between what the client now wants and what we had previously agreed to?" That tends to put me in a problem-solving frame of mind and I can take the client along the path with me.

John: Yep. That is probably something that will work with Johnson.

Paul: I think it will. What I have found, John—see what you think about this—is that most people just want to be heard. Some clients can get all their thoughts out in one swoop and one neat contract. Others need you to stop and help them catch up at every meeting. How might you incorporate this in your next meeting with Johnson?

John: As you said, sometimes it just means making a minor adjustment, and other times I might need to say, "I really like that idea and I believe it will make the product stronger. It will mean two more weeks of production that I will need to add to the contract. Is this OK with you, or would you like to rethink how we might go about this?"

Paul: Exactly. That's how I would handle it. Is this helpful? How might you take this and apply it to reduce your frustration and get closer to the result you are seeking?

John: I'm meeting with Johnson on Friday. I'm definitely going to try it. It should work until the next frustration comes along! Thanks, Paul.

Paul: Sounds good. I'll come by on Monday to find out how it went. Given that I haven't worked with Johnson before, maybe you can share some additional tips with me!

In what ways is this conversation more powerful than the preceding conversation? Notice the use of questions and active listening that is apparent between John and Paul. Consider the ways in which they convey respect and support. In talking through this challenge, Paul makes it clear that he is interested in helping John. John shares his concerns and frustrations. Paul helps him move beyond those concerns and frustrations to finding a way forward. What would it be like if everyone worked in an organization in which the conversations were like this? Engagement and performance would be high, business conversations would be marked by a solution focus and mutual support, and goals and objectives would be more readily met.

That isn't to imply we believe that all social institutions and companies should follow this organizational environment. We are not passing judgment in terms of right or wrong. Rather, we are supporting what the research has proven to be the kind of culture that leads to engagement, award-winning workplaces, increased profits, bottom-line goal achievement, longevity and sustainability, respected leadership, and supported followership. We are talking about learning organizations in which human interactions and structures are created to help people and the organization realize hidden potential.

Obviously, this doesn't just happen. In fact, it never ends. It is a continuous journey of learning. As Peter Senge describes, it is in these types of organizations "where people continually expand their capacity to create the results they truly desire, where new and expansive patterns of thinking are nurtured, where collective aspiration is set free, and where people are continually learning how to learn together" (1990, 3). Dialogue and the right conversations serve this purpose.

This theme of dialogue and the right conversations being able to create high-performing organizations can be noted in the writings of dozens of experts over the years; further, it is steeped in theory and practice, tested over time.

The Importance of Mindful Dialogue

In the early 1990s, Daniel Goleman began to write about the importance of emotional intelligence (EI) in the workplace. He cited that organizations in which leaders displayed EI were rated higher as positive places to work than those without it. He stressed that EI leaders express appropriate feelings and direction through mindful dialogue.

Ten years later, when Goleman shared research that demonstrated that EI workplaces were not only rated as the best places to work but also the most profitable, the adoption of EI exploded. In essence, the "soft stuff" was the answer for achieving the "hard stuff" (Goleman 2000). The vehicle for attaining these results are coaching conversations and behaviors, such as asking questions, testing assumptions, and listening intently. In particular, Goleman (1998) talks about giving frequent feedback, encouraging practice, arranging support, providing models, reinforcing positive behaviors, and evaluating success. Sound familiar? The Seven Cs Coaching Map comes to mind.

Some think that EI means sharing your emotions as part of an ongoing sensitivity training. Not so. Rather, leaders and people in organizations learn to use and manage their emotions to create better organizations, because everything in human interaction involves emotions, whether they are spoken or not. If they are spoken openly, nonthreateningly, they lead to problem solving and collaboration. When they are hidden, they sneak out through sabotage, politics, backstabbing, and hostility.

Real conversations are the inner ones; once surfaced constructively, team-work and productive action emerge. This is not easy to achieve. It means using a language that cuts through hidden agendas, control, fear, resentments, and other barriers that prevent people from sharing the reasoning behind their words and actions. Using real dialogue results in trust and support. But old habits are hard to break. And when an entire company has learned to talk in "defensive routines," it takes the commitment of leaders who want to create coaching environments to establish more productive forms of communication.

In her book *The Last Word on Power*, Tracy Goss traces the importance of language back to the philosopher Heidegger (1996, 19):

> Language is the only leverage for changing the context of the world around you. This is because people apprehend and construct reality through the way they speak and listen. Or, as Martin Heidegger put it: "Language is the house of being." On a day to day basis you can alter the way you are *being* by altering the conversations in which you are engaged.

Like Heidegger, Goss emphasizes the word *being* to indicate not only a purpose and frame of mind, but a way of life. She points out that by uncovering aspects of your conversations and learning to engage in different types of conversations, you can alter the way you are being, which in turn, alters what's possible. This new "space of living" (sometimes referred to as "presence") alters the way you approach language and interactions. Instead of talking with the intent of disagreeing, proving, or judging, you listen with the intent of openness, knowledge, curiosity, and learning. In approaching a conversation with the intent of discovery as opposed to judging, how might results be improved? Revisit the scenario between Paul and John for an example.

Continuing our language journey, Robert Goodman (2002) writes about "constructive developmentalism" and "developmental coaching dialogue" and uses the early work of Jean Piaget and Robert Kegan to explain the mind's ability to use language to develop increased complexity in thought and action. He cites coaching examples with executives and demonstrates how coaching language can change thinking and behavior. When you helped Gail assess her own situation, reflect on the results she wanted, and formulate her own actions and results, she reached a higher level of thinking for future decisions. You created a space in which Gail could step back from her own reality, reframe that reality into one with action, and re-engage with a different perspective and result. You became a bridge to higher performance. In a coaching organization, everyone becomes a bridge for one another.

Alan Sieler (2016), founder of the Newfield Institute, describes organizations as a "network of conversations." He uses the often-quoted words of Truett Anderson to sum up the powerful connection between language and organizations: "Organisations are linguistic structures built out of words and maintained by conversations. Even problems that aren't strictly communicational—failures of mechanical systems for example—can be explored in terms of things said and not said, questions asked and not asked, conversations never begun or left uncompleted, alternative explanations not discussed."

The What and Why of Coaching Conversations

Let's step back and pull a few pieces together. To create coaching conversations and cultures, we hone our language using a conversational approach that encourages the reasoning behind our words to be made evident; namely, dialogue. Then we add the Seven Cs Coaching Map—with accompanying coaching tools and approaches. What we end up with are "coaching conversations," the major ingredient for building coaching cultures.

Using a coaching approach in everyday conversations can support colleagues, surface hidden agendas, create centers of collaboration, and foster higher levels of success and achievement. There are three primary reasons for the recent popularity of coaching in organizations:

1. Coaching provides greater potential for learning and practicing new behaviors than other forms of learning.
2. Coaching is personal—a person receives tailored attention and dialogue for his needs and goals. This provides a centered, focused approach that makes the individual feel empowered.
3. Coaching can happen face-to-face or virtually. It can keep up with the pace of today's working populations.

Many global coaching studies and surveys (which will be covered in detail in part 3) have found that coaching:

- can measure and lead to meaningful return on investment and organizational effectiveness
- assignments most frequently deal with change (organizational and personal)

- develops high potentials, facilitates transitions, and successfully addresses derailing behavior
- leads to positive social results.

With research proving the positive effects of coaching in organizations, company leaders should consider multiple coaching avenues to enhance not only key individuals but entire teams, departments, and institutions. Classic one-on-one professional coaching must continue as a vehicle for change. Leaders, directors, and managers can be coached toward behaviors and skill sets needed for the future of the enterprise and their personal growth. They then become role models for the rest of the organization and begin to inspire meetings with more purposeful conversations. In addition, using a coaching approach in everyday conversations can support colleagues, surface hidden insights, create collaboration centers, and reach higher levels of success.

Coaching Definitions

We've mentioned a few examples of coaching dialogue, both formal and informal. Now let's review some classic coaching definitions:

- "Conversations to help and support people to take responsibility for managing their own learning and change" (Parsloe and Leedham 2016).
- "Coaching is unlocking people's potential to maximize their own performance" (Whitmore 2011).
- "An interactive process to help individuals and organizations develop more rapidly and produce more satisfying results" (ICF 2016).
- "Challenging and supporting people in achieving higher levels of performance while allowing them to bring out the best in themselves and those around them" (Hargrove 1995).
- "A Socratic based future focused dialogue between a facilitator (coach) and a participant (coachee or client) where the facilitator uses open questions, active listening, summaries and reflections which are aimed at stimulating self-awareness and personal responsibility of the participant" (Passmore and Fillery-Travis 2011).

Commonalities in these definitions are such concepts as learning, potential, performance, self-awareness, and results. These are words of strength and possibility.

Anyone who decides to create a coaching culture needs to have a vision and a plan. Consider what coaching is not and ensure coordination with other systems within an organization. Table 1-2 shows the similarities and differences between coaching and other learning practices. Note that coaching is future focused, individualized, and tailored. It uses powerful questions, data to deepen the learning, and personal accountability. At times, there may be overlap—for example, a mentor may also be trained as a coach—but other strategies tend to come from a "fix it" or "expert" mentality (consulting or therapy) or address more generic learning. With coaching, it is the diligent use of straight talk, inquiry, and listening—and the surfacing of hidden reasoning and potential—that drives the process of discovery and action.

Table 1-2. Coaching and Other Behavioral Strategies

Practice	Focus
Coaching	Supports individuals or teams in realizing their full potential. Emphasizes self-awareness and growth.
Consulting	Addresses problems by diagnosing situations and prescribing solutions; assumes the consultant is the expert.
Training	Focuses on specific skills and content; usually involves a shorter timeframe than coaching. Content may be delivered in person or virtually, to a group or one-on-one.
Mentoring	Occurs often between senior and junior employees for career development; emphasizes organizational goals and advice.
Therapy	Focuses on problems, pathologies, and healing. Emphasis on understanding the past and origins of feelings.
Facilitating	Emphasizes immediate problem solving or long-term effectiveness; supports group reflection on what they're doing and why.

Bianco-Mathis, Nabors, and Roman (2002)

This process can happen in structured coaching sessions with a certified coach, or in more unstructured situations, such as a manager speaking with an employee. Table 1-3 demonstrates this continuum and provides examples.

Table 1-3. Coaching Continuum

Examples	External Coach Practitioner	Internal Coach Practitioner	HR or Organization Development Professional Using Coaching Skills or Language	Manager or Leader Using Coaching Skills or Language	Colleague Using Coaching Skills or Language
Structured Coaching Examples	Tony, the chief financial officer, selects a credentialed coach (Walt) from his organization's coaching pool. They create and sign a coaching agreement that details roles and responsibilities, logistics, and parameters of confidentiality. The coaching agenda is informed by Tony's recent 360-degree feedback and his intention to strengthen his leadership skills.	Susan and Brian, managers who have received coaching training, are assigned to provide coaching support to the members of the emerging leaders cohort in their association. The support is for a set period. They use a short, written agreement to describe the coaching partnership so that their coachees understand how this work is different from training or mentoring. Elisa, an organization development manager, is working with Paul to help him strengthen his skills in providing timely, accurate feedback to his employees. When they began their work, Elisa explained the coaching process to Paul and they talked through what he wanted to achieve. They both signed a coaching agreement and Paul drafted an action plan that they review periodically.	Kathy, a certified coach, supports a newly formed team as they plan and implement new technology. She is a part of their biweekly meetings and as agreed, shares her observations of behavior in the meetings to support team learning. Jill, the learning and development manager in a small association, provides onboarding coaching support to Vern, a new accounting manager, for 120 days. This includes scheduled meetings and a planned agenda that Vern can adjust as questions or issues come up.	Diane meets with her staff for scheduled monthly check-ins. She makes it clear that she is wearing her "coaching hat" when she supports them with results-focused conversations that leverage and acknowledge their progress toward agreed-upon objectives, and she helps them consider options for moving forward if they get stuck. She "asks" more than she "tells." She clarifies what action her team members will take before the next meeting.	Meaghan, a long-tenured employee who has completed a coaching program, agrees to help Nigel, a newly promoted employee, for four months. Nigel has proposed an agenda where he can talk through ideas and test interpretations of the unwritten rules in the organization.

Unstructured Coaching Examples	Jenn, a senior marketing executive, calls her former coach, Teri. She asks if Teri has a minute to listen to a situation. Jenn shares a current opportunity she is considering and walks Teri through her thought process demonstrating some of the skills she acquired during their coaching work. Teri acknowledges her thorough approach.	Chong, an operations manager, accepts her colleague Alan's invitation to attend his staff meeting and provide feedback on his facilitating. Afterward, while walking to their next meeting, Chong shares her observations and asks a few questions that help Alan identify the impact of his behavior on his team.	David, a training manager, is having lunch with Marla, a budget analyst. She shares that she is struggling to plan and deliver performance feedback for one of her staff. David asks questions that help Marla focus on what she wants to accomplish and what approach is most likely to yield her desired results. He reminds her of her commitment to develop her staff, which he has heard her say many times. He asks her how delivering the feedback supports that commitment.	When team members drop by his office looking for answers in areas where they have experience, Sam uses powerful questions to help them expand their thinking and consider different approaches.	Jamal observes Linda in their weekly meeting and notices that she is uncharacteristically quiet. As they leave the meeting, he asks, "What's going on?" Linda shares her concern with an upcoming conversation with her boss. She says she just can't organize her thoughts. Jamal asks, "How helpful would it be if I coach you?" With Linda's permission, Jamal asks a number of questions that help her identify what she wants to accomplish in the upcoming conversation.

Whether it is a formal coaching situation over several months or a quick coaching conversation in the company cafeteria, the Seven Cs Coaching Map can be utilized to fully move thoughts and feelings to action. While part 2 provides many examples for each step, Table 1-1 provides a broad over-view to guide your reading. The following case scenario (Bianco-Mathis and Nabors 2015) can be used to demonstrate the concepts in Table 1-1.

Gail was a sales manager in charge of eight sales representatives across the Mid-Atlantic region. She was becoming frustrated because she would visit clients with each of her sales reps on a regular basis and then give advice and feedback. Unfortunately, when she returned on her next trip, she would note that the sales reps still made some of the same mistakes that she had pointed out previously. Having hired the group herself, she knows they are bright and have the right sales skills. She also knows they are overworked and find it difficult to organize their daily visits and paperwork—in addition to incor-porating all her advice. Having attended an informative workshop on how to implement coaching into her management style, she decides to develop a more mindful approach. She studied her coaching materials and created worksheets, action plans, customer feedback sheets, and tracking sheets as aids she could use in meeting with each rep.

Capture Context

Gail met with each of her representatives and explained that she wanted to start using a coaching approach to help reps reach their potential. She also described the method as being "less telling" and using more questioning, role playing, suggesting, offering of ideas, committing to actions, journaling, updating action plans, and reflecting on results. Gail also encouraged each rep to be fully present for each meeting and that she was going to be more focused in analyzing actions and results. Gail described her role as that of a guide and partner as she and her reps sought to improve the performance of the division.

At this initial meeting, Gail asked each rep to personally commit to the process and to follow some ground rules; for example, "Either party will give 24-hour notice if a meeting needs to be canceled" and, "Both parties will come to each meeting fully prepped." Gail also asked reps to reflect on their performance over the last six months and to discuss strengths and areas where they would like to improve. She also shared her thoughts and tested those against each rep's perception. To accomplish this, she used powerful questions such as:

- What do you believe you do well as a rep?
- Walk me through a couple of scenarios of interacting with your clients and how you exhibit your strengths.
- What strategies do you use to do that well?
- Now let's imagine it is six months from now. What would you like to do even better? Play that out for me.

By using such behavioral dialogue, Gail was able to develop general areas to explore for coaching.

Clarify Purpose and Collect and Feed Back Data

Based on the information in her initial discussions, Gail gave each rep a worksheet to further define areas of coaching exploration and to analyze available data to home in on more specific objectives. As it turned out, each rep had just been given a 360-degree inventory on key job competencies and had also just received performance appraisals. Thus, the worksheet provided instructions on how to review these documents and extract and prioritize strengths and areas to improve. At the next session with each rep, Gail reviewed the worksheets and, through dialogue, highlighted two items—key areas to work on, and existing strengths—that could be leveraged in working on the areas to explore.

Create Options

In the same meeting—or for some reps, in a couple of meetings—Gail used dialogue to further explore each area:

- How can you improve the way you negotiate with the store managers?
- What would you have to do to fit this into your schedule?
- What resources could help you?
- What's your goal? Share with me a picture of you being a great negotiator.
- How long do you think it would take to reach such a goal? Consider the fact that you can't just jump from OK negotiator to fantastic negotiator. What are some benchmarks you can incorporate?

- What are you apprehensive about regarding negotiation? How might you overcome those apprehensions?
- What would happen if you never improved your negotiation skills?

Gail noted that the conversation tended to be different with each rep: Some jumped into the exploration with both feet, while some needed more encouragement and pacing in terms of developing the future picture. Some of the reps needed a more iterative, back-and-forth approach, while others needed to be held back from taking on too much. With each conversation, Gail found it easier to ask questions and create dialogue. What was hard for her was moving from "telling" to "supporting and offering."

Construct a Plan and Commit to Action

As Gail continued to meet with her reps, she guided each to develop a clear plan of action, including each area to explore, specific objectives within that area, desired results, steps to achieve those results, a benchmarked timeline, measures and criteria to ascertain achievement, supporting resources to assist the process, and actual "field practice" that would be done in between each follow-up meeting. Here is a typical example of this process:

> **Gail:** I agree, working on negotiation skills would up your game in the way you have described. We have mapped out a three-month process for that to happen and discussed several activities that you can undertake and try. What can you try between now and our next meeting in two weeks?
>
> **Joe:** Well, given that we homed in on the particular aspect of negotiation I want to master—specifically "brainstorming win-win strategies"—it would behoove me to concentrate on that.
>
> **Gail:** Very good point. What resources do you have at your disposal to improve your skills?
>
> **Joe:** Steven is excellent at this. I'd like to spend a day with him and just watch him.
>
> **Gail:** I like the idea of you spending time with Steven. What could you do to make that as productive as possible?

Joe: I'd like to review the negotiating module from the training we had a year ago and pinpoint four or five behaviors that support my area of need. Then maybe I can share those with Steven and let him know I'll be looking for those. I think I'd also like to develop a list of win-win alternatives by conducting a focus group with various sales teams throughout the company. It might also be possible for me to attend a more focused course on negotiation. The one we attended was broad in nature.

Gail: Those are all excellent ideas. What else could you do?

(Gail and Joe continue to work this through.)

Gail: Great. Summarize for me what you are committing to make happen before our next meeting. Joe: All right, let's see. I'm going to review the negotiation module and have a phone call with Tanya, who is excellent at negotiating deals. From the data, I am going to create a checklist of activities and behaviors I want to share with Steven, note what Steven does during the time I shadow him, and then spend an hour with him at the end of the day, reflecting on my notes. From there, I am going to develop a job aid that I will then use for my next three sales visits and note the results in my journal for implementing those new techniques. We will discuss that at our next meeting and then decide on next steps I can take to further my learning, practice, and results. Wow! That is what I am committing to!

Gail: Yes. Exactly. How do you feel about this plan?

As it turned out, Joe struggled a bit with mastering negotiation skills. With further conversations, it became evident that Joe was working from the belief that meeting the customer's need was the most important element of the sale; thus, he found it difficult to move from an either/or to a both/and mindset. Once he addressed this, he began to improve his negotiation skills. Gail realized that Joe's improvement could never have happened if she had used her old method of "Hey Joe, you have to get better at negotiation."

Celebrate Success

After three months, Gail noted that all her reps were demonstrating real achievement, not mere surface results. As her team improved, she was able to reduce the number of coaching sessions to one every two months and to implement an innovative once-a-month team coaching session. The following dialogue between Gail and Joe demonstrates the celebrating success approach:

> **Gail:** So how has it been going the past two weeks? What went well?
>
> **Joe:** It's been going well. All three of my customer interactions resulted in a win-win result. It's the first time I felt totally confident and wasn't hesitating or second-guessing myself.
>
> **Gail:** That's terrific. So, on a scale from 1 (low) to 10 (high), how confident do you feel about your negotiation skills?
>
> **Joe:** Definitely an 8.
>
> **Gail:** Do you remember how you rated yourself three months ago?
>
> **Joe:** Ha. I think I thought I was about a 3.
>
> **Gail:** Yep. That's exactly what you said. Let's review the action steps you have taken since then. Look at this summary column in your action plan. What goes through your mind as you review your progress?
>
> **Joe:** Seeing it all laid out like this, I'm impressed with the progress I've made. It was hard work. I look at this notation—I really botched that interaction, remember? I'm so much stronger now.
>
> **Gail:** What lessons have you learned about yourself from having gone through this process?

Making this coaching transition won't come easy to everyone. Even though you might conceptually see how this model works, you might be wondering how to manage an individual coaching meeting. How do I begin? What do I say? How do I know when to move on to actions or commitment? We've been asked this question many times, and we developed the C-O-A-CH meeting model as a result (Table 1-4). Within one typical traditional coaching meeting—or within one "coaching on the fly" conversation as we saw with Gail at the beginning of this chapter—using the C-O-A-CH model will ensure that you cover the major steps to help people move to action.

Table 1-4. C-O-A-CH Model

Steps	Example
Step 1: Current situation—Describe and explore data, feedback, and client's perceptions. The emphasis is on gaining mutual understanding of the current reality as it is perceived by the client and others. Getting mutual clarity on the current situation is necessary to establish clear, realistic objectives for development.	**Question:** What strengths do you see in your 360-degree feedback? **Statement:** Provide an example in which you have used your strengths to your advantage.
Step 2: Objectives—Define coaching goals, desired results, and measurable objectives (for a particular meeting and for the overall coaching process). Objectives may take into account individual, team, and organizational needs.	**Question:** What would you like to achieve in today's coaching meeting? **Statement:** Tell me what you believe a successful or valuable result of today's meeting would be.
Step 3: Alternatives—Explore alternative approaches and ideas for how to reach the designated objectives. Brainstorming and exploration of feelings and reasoning are part of the coaching conversation.	**Question:** What are three ways you might approach this opportunity? **Statement:** That is one solution. Help me understand how it meets your overall objective.
Step 4: CHoices—Support the client as he makes choices for action, including next steps, milestones, and other elements of a coaching action plan.	**Question:** How would you like to move forward? **Statement:** Walk me through your plan for next steps.

As you can see, this model collapses the overall coaching map into four distinct steps that are easy to remember as you move through the flow of a meaningful conversation. In applying the model to the Gail and Joe role play just covered, you can see how Gail moved through all four steps in only a short dialogue:

C: Gail wanted to help Joe get better at negotiation.

O: Gail and Joe set an objective of mastering the negotiation component of brainstorming alternatives.

A: Gail and Joe brainstormed ideas to reach his objective, such as reviewing course materials, talking to Tanya, shadowing Steven, making a list of observation points, conducting a focus group, and attending a more specific course.

CH: Gail supported Joe in making choices to move forward.

When you are coaching in the moment or over time, you may find it helpful to keep this shorter model in mind. If you ever find yourself getting stuck, you just say, "OK, where am I? Yes, I should now move to 'alternatives.'" C-O-A-CH helps you track and punctuate the key components of the coaching conversation so the coachee begins to internalize the same thinking frame for continuous self-improvement.

Incorporating Coaching in an Organization

As chapter 8 will show, an organizational leader needs to choose to build a coaching organization. This then becomes part of the organization's vision, values, and ways of behaving. This drives organizational processes such as team behavior, appraisal systems, strategic planning, leadership and managerial development, and decision making. Through both formal and informal mechanisms, coaching becomes the expected way of communicating and getting things done. The manifestation of this might be implemented through many different channels:

- frequent learning sessions led by managers and staff alike
- storytelling of the best and worst client experiences over the last month
- partner feedback sessions on getting a project out
- quarterly upward feedback
- software programs encouraging easy and daily feedback between managers and teams
- weekly analysis of agreed-upon metrics for continuous improvement
- pool of certified internal and external coaches
- innovative rewards for breakthrough thinking.

The creative avenues are limited only by the amount of dialogue encouraged.

To end this chapter, let's return to the powerful use of dialogue and the cognitive theories behind mindful conversations. Language is hardwired in our brains as a part of our neurolinguistic programming. Neuroscience and ontology have added many tools and exercises that support coaches in their work. These tools are effective in helping clients create new pathways in their brains, sidestepping less useful behaviors, and instead pursuing more effective behaviors.

David Rock (2009) explains that trying to change someone's behavior is like trying to change the path of the river at the bottom of the Grand Canyon. That path has been established over centuries, just as our neurological pathways have been forged through generations. So what do we do? Rock suggests that we help people build bridges over the engrained pathways and encourage individuals to practice how to stop, recognize the new pathway, and then choose that new pathway to more readily use a new behavior. Like adopting any new behavior—such as mastering a tennis swing or writing an essay—it takes repetition, feedback, reinforcement, and time. It takes an action plan, support of a coach, continuous practice, and adjustments until the new behavior becomes just as natural as the flow of a very old river.

To better understand what goes on in a person's brain through coaching, see Table 1-5. As soon as a coach starts using dialogue—indicating curiosity and openness as opposed to judgment and blame—an atmosphere of openness is established. The listener responds honestly and doesn't become defensive. Both parties are then free to share their reasoning, test assumptions, and explore possibilities, creating a pool of knowledge, perspective, and insights. Blinders are removed, and there is access to previously unseen alternatives. As dialogue continues, opportunities, alternative behaviors, new windows, and innovative actions emerge. Soon, the coach asks for a choice and declaration of action. The coachee trusts the situation, commits to a series of actions, continues to practice, takes accountability, and gets closer to the desired future picture. (See the appendix for an example of deconstructing dialogue with the role play between Paul and John.)

Table 1-5. Deconstructing Dialogue

When You:	You Demonstrate:	Resulting In:
Establish a coaching context	Interest, positive intent, and a learning focus	A safe space for open conversation and reflection
Help identify desired results	A future focus and interest in coaching outcomes	A vision of the future and workable action plan with tangible measures
Listen and ask powerful questions	Care, curiosity, and support	Questioning assumptions and considering new perspectives and behaviors
Consider alternative perspectives	Flexibility and outward thinking	More choices, greater skill in perspective taking, and increased buy-in

Table 1-5. Deconstructing Dialogue (cont.)

When You:	You Demonstrate:	Resulting In:
Request a declaration of action	Confidence and a focus on moving forward	Movement with purpose and a spotlight on what can be done
Talk through and capture lessons learned	Openness and interest in continuous learning	Shared information, commitment to higher levels of performance, and increased skill sets

Making It Real

This chapter discussed language, dialogue, and the science and art of "changing the conversation." If you follow the Seven Cs Coaching Map and the C-O-A-CH model, your conversations can enable insights, openness, solutions, and trust to emerge. Please reflect on this chapter and develop ideas for how to incorporate what you learned into your work.

Imagine a difficult conversation that didn't go as well as desired.

1. Describe the conversation in terms of the flow, tone, approach, and outcomes; also indicate some of the language that was used.
   - Difficult conversation scenario:

   - Difficult conversation language:

2. Based on what you read in this chapter, develop a goal for how the conversation could have been better handled, and an example of language that could have been applied using the C-O-A-CH model.
   - Goal:

   - Alternative language:
     - C:

     - O:

     - A:

     - CH:

2

Dialogue—Learning the Language of Coaching

As described in chapter 1, dialogue is a way of engaging in conversation for creating greater understanding. Dialogue enables effective communication by changing the rhythm and flow of conversation. As William Isaacs (1999) describes, when people are practicing dialogue, they are involved in a conversation with a center, not sides, channeling their energy into creating something new. The experience is centered on expanding understanding such that all parties come away with a greater appreciation of perspective—theirs and others. Dialogue supports individuals, teams, and organizations to more effectively solve problems, trust others, and learn.

If dialogue offers such a substantive array of benefits, why don't more people use it? First, skill sets must be learned, and many people have convinced themselves that they don't have time to do so. Second, practicing dialogue requires courage—a willingness to admit that you don't know everything and that you are willing to be informed by others to come up with the most complete answer or solution. Third, dialogue requires an interest in and an awareness of others that some of us have not yet learned to practice. So, how are people communicating?

My World, My Way

In the 1970s, Chris Argyris introduced what he called "the ladder of inference" to describe the process by which humans process information and come to conclusions. Since that time, other authors have proposed similar models to explain how we move from experiencing an event to reacting to that event. These authors and others agree on the following:

1. Something happens.
2. We tell ourselves a story about what happened (related partially, wholly, or not at all to the facts).
3. We feel a certain way.
4. We act based on those feelings.

It is important to note that this entire process takes only seconds to complete and we are largely unaware of each separate step. Also, the story we tell ourselves (step 2) generally supports our beliefs about ourselves and others (and is incomplete). Consider this example:

> **Something happens:** You are in the conference room preparing for your team meeting. You are scheduled to present a run-through of your recommendations to the team's executive sponsor, Kevin. Kevin sticks his head into the conference room and says, "Something has come up and I won't be joining you today. Good luck with the run-through." And he leaves.
>
> **We tell ourselves a story:** You think, "Wow, Kevin must not be that interested in this project after all."
>
> **The story allows us to feel a certain way:** You feel disrespected and angry at Kevin. The team worked really hard to come up with a creative solution to the logistics challenge you faced, and he doesn't even have time to hear it? He was never in favor of this initiative anyway. Well, you don't need him.
>
> **We act based on those feelings:** When the team comes in, you tell them that Kevin isn't interested in your recommendation and you'd better reach out to other executive team members to line up their support.

In this case, Kevin is cast as the villain. By definition, you are cast as the heroine. The interpretation of the events and the meaning you assign to them may be completely off base. And yet, it is your interpretation and you are ready to take it forward as though it were gospel.

These interpretations and the following actions happen every day, and we often don't stop to question our "understanding" of any given event. Add to this natural human habit the changes in technology that have made access to information almost immediate. Now you can share your "understanding" of any given event in a text, a tweet, or an email. You can post it on Facebook or LinkedIn. You can blog about it. The more opportunity you have to tell your story, the more attached to it you become, and the less likely you are to consider an alternative storyline.

Given these circumstances, it is not surprising that effective communication between individuals, among team members, and within organizations is rare. In our haste to make sense of situations quickly, multitask, and meet the implicit or explicit expectations for speedy responses, most of our communication is flawed. Misunderstanding, misinterpretation, and assumptions based on partial or outdated information all lead to mistakes, rework, and weakened connections with colleagues, stakeholders, suppliers, and the public. So, what can you do?

Slow Down

To start, you can increase the space you have between an event and your rush to action. You can allow yourself to respond rather than react to that event. The first step is to acknowledge that you control the space that exists between an action and your reaction. You can choose to enlarge that space. You can choose to adopt a learning stance and ask questions such as:

- What happened here?
- What does this mean?
- How might someone else look at this?
- What can I learn here?
- How did I contribute to this?

Asking these questions takes time and slows down the action. The next step is to explore your feelings about the event rather than accepting them at face value:

- How do I feel about this?
- What is making me feel this way?
- How else can I feel?
- What is the benefit and cost of these feelings?

Finally, you can choose a response and act accordingly. Questions to consider at this point are:

- What result do I want to achieve?
- How does this behavior bring me closer to my desired result?
- How else can I respond?
- What are the benefits and costs of responding this way?

Of course, you do not work through these steps alone. You are generally interacting with others, so the opportunity exists to involve other people in sorting through these thoughts. You can do this by inquiring, or asking questions of them to find out what they intended and how they experienced the interaction. You can also share your feelings or thoughts and test them out. In other words, you can clarify what you want or expect and see how closely that matches with what the other person wants or expects. As long as you are both putting information on the table, you have the chance to create a shared understanding and agreements on how you will move forward. This way, your actions are "informed" and, generally speaking, more complete. The key to this process is effectively using the skills of dialogue.

Rewriting the Script

In most Western workplaces, discussion is the most common mode of communication. Convincing others is valued and so people work to persuade, convince, defend, sell, or tell others. Individuals focus on specific parts of an issue and focus their thinking on that part, with little or no consideration of the touchpoints with the other parts that make up the whole. Information is shared in a segmented manner, influenced by politics and a desired outcome, making it difficult to consider the issue in its entirety and all its ramifications.

Think of the last time you were in a meeting. How many statements did you hear, compared with the number of questions asked? Most meeting participants report statements outnumbering questions by a wide margin. Proclaiming the benefit of a course of action and arguing in support of it promotes a win/lose dynamic that characterizes many meetings. Getting your way is valued in many situations, and the short-term gain is often overshadowed by long-term costs such as unexpected consequences, redundancies, and uninformed thinking.

Compare this modality of communication with dialogue. Creating space within which dialogue is valued and practiced yields positive, substantive results. Participants learn from one another, and overall they are better informed. Teams and organizations that use dialogue consistently make better decisions and experience greater learning and increased profitability. Although there is an initial investment of time required to learn dialogue skills, teams that do so are able to work more quickly, and more people become better decision makers.

The Dialogue Building Blocks

Dialogue requires a shift in the way many leaders and managers have learned their roles. It requires looking beyond yourself and using the type of "outward mindset" that puts others first and demonstrates a genuine curiosity and solution focus (Arbinger Institute 2016). It requires a level of courage and care: courage to allow others to see that you may not have all the answers, and care in asking others to inform your thinking and then listening when they do so. It also requires a facility with seven building blocks, or skill areas, to effectively navigate the powerful stream of meaning that dialogue creates.

Let's look at these seven building blocks and see how you can incorporate them into your conversations. Table 2-1 offers some benefits of each building block for you and others with whom you interact.

Table 2-1. Benefits of the Dialogue Building Blocks

Building Block	Benefit to You	Benefit to Others
Focus	» Clarifies desired outcome » Highlights intention; enables attention	» Creates a clear purpose for the conversation » Outlines what to expect
Listen	» Supports data gathering » Deepens understanding	» Conveys respect » Creates a partnership
Question	» Demonstrates curiosity » Surfaces commonality and differences	» Provokes further thinking » Encourages solutions that go beyond the surface
Reveal	» Exposes thinking and rationale » Invites additional data	» Expands other's perception of you » Deepens understanding
Challenge	» Expands perspective	» Demonstrates openness
Negotiate	» Presents clear objectives » Revisits intention	» Highlights areas on which to build » Encourages stronger solutions
Commit	» Captures promises made » Clarifies next steps	» Captures promises made » Clarifies next steps

Used with permission from Bianco-Mathis and Nabors (2015)

Building Block 1: Focus

Before having any important conversation, it is vital to consider what you want the outcome to be when the conversation is over. In other words, if you envision having the conversation and it goes well, what does that look like? What is the result? What is the agreement that has been reached? How do you (or the other person) feel about the outcome? You can consider these questions as you prepare for the conversation. They will help you become centered and concentrate on achieving the results you have defined as "successful." Consider the following examples.

Cynthia is the general counsel for a small, not-for-profit organization. She is passionate about their mission and her responsibility to mitigate risks when it comes to public interactions. She has seen the marketing department play fast and loose with the requirements for signed releases in the past, and the new vice president of marketing, Steve, seems to be reading from the same playbook. She has tried to speak with him (unsuccessfully) in the past, and now his staff are following his lead.

Cynthia wants to prepare for a coaching conversation and focus on what she is trying to achieve. She does not want to get distracted by personal attacks or off-topic references. She prepares a short state-ment of her desired outcome: "I will successfully convey the risk to the organization of not obtaining signed releases, and marketing will commit to obtaining signed releases in every case in which we want to publish photos. My personal relationship with Steve will be strength-ened through our conversation. On a scale of 1-10, these outcomes are a 10 to me." By clarifying her desired outcomes, Cynthia can keep her attention where it needs to be and is less likely to be sidetracked by any excuses or attacks Steve throws her way.

Charles is the team lead for the newly formed branch chiefs' council. He's noticed that the council members are sidetracked when agenda items come up that will affect one of their specific areas. He wants to help the team stay on track, so he revisits their team charter and extracts their purpose statement. It reads, "We intend to act as a collaborative body, bringing a horizontal focus to issues that cross division lines in service to the agency overall." Charles decides to post this purpose state-ment and refer members to it when the conversation takes too much of a siloed turn. By posting the team's purpose statement, Charles creates a visual reminder he can refer to whenever the council goes off track.

In both examples, the focus building block supports purposeful conversation in service to a desired outcome. Clarifying that outcome helps all parties stay on track and course correct when necessary.

Building Block 2: Listen

Most people are not good listeners. They are distracted from what the other person is saying by many things: their own thoughts, background noise, feelings, conflicting information, and so on. Effective listening is a critical skill, one that can be developed if you are truly interested in improving the quality of your communication with others.

When you prepare for an important conversation, you likely will make a few notes about the points you want to convey and what you'd like to learn. Making notes helps you to free your thoughts so that you can concentrate more fully on what the other person is saying. You can pay attention to how closely the person's verbal and nonverbal messaging align. You can consider the extent to which what the person is saying matches her previous messages on the subject and to what extent it is new information.

The following example illustrates that listening is a key part of the process of sharing and discovering information that will lead to effective coaching moments.

Mark is a deputy chief information officer (CIO) in a midsize government agency. He has a remarkable skill set that combines strategic acumen and tactical expertise. He can see alternatives and answers when many others are stuck. Surprisingly, this gets him into trouble. Rather than acknowledging points that have been made by colleagues or referencing commitments that have been given, Mark will often share his thinking by saying, "We could just do XYZ." This stand-alone commentary makes it seem as though he hasn't listened to what others have said or that he has and he just doesn't care.

Working with a coach, Mark came to realize the impact of this behavior, so he developed some new approaches. He started to acknowledge points that others made, enabling him to clearly convey that he was listening. Then he raised his points framed as questions to consider, "How might it work if . . ." or, "I wonder how it could help if. . . ." Over time, Mark's colleagues felt heard by him and came to appreciate his questions as contributing to better outcomes. He demonstrates his listening in a purposeful way and his colleagues feel respected. Creating a partnership with colleagues allows Mark to credibly raise questions in service to a goal bigger than himself.

Building Block 3: Question

Powerful questions can move you beyond the surface in a conversation. They can help you identify real issues and feelings (yours and others') that have to be considered to problem solve and craft meaningful solutions. Frame questions so they go beyond "yes" and "no" answers. Encourage the other person to help you understand why they think or feel the way they do. The more information you collect, the greater chance you have of recognizing your areas of commonality. Consider the following examples.

Jessica is a talented chief financial officer (CFO) of a midsize organization. The organization's board wants to involve her more in a key financing project. However, Jessica doesn't have time because throughout the day her staff are coming to her with questions regarding their work, and she answers them. Over time, Jessica has reinforced this behavior. After talking over her intention to change this behavior with her coach, Jessica tried the following. She committed to asking at least three questions before she gave anyone answers. She decided upon the three questions she would most likely use, and she kept them posted in her office.

After one week, she reported to her coach that her staff were laughing at her. When her coach asked her how she wanted to proceed, Jessica agreed to keep going until their next scheduled meeting, which was a week away. At the meeting, Jessica told her coach, "They've stopped laughing. More important, when they come in, they are now asking a question and then sharing with me one or two strategies and ideas they have to solve their problem. And most of the time they are exactly on target. I can't believe the change in only two weeks."

Margaret felt as though she was reliving the same moment over and over. Once again, she received a work product from Leslie's group and it wasn't what she had asked for. She remembered explicitly requesting the promotional material to be formatted for mobile devices. What she was looking at was a print media format, which was not useful for mobile devices. How did this happen? She resisted the urge to pick up the phone and just give Leslie a piece of her mind. She thought about how she could get more information. What questions could she ask that could help her understand how this happened and, more important, how could she be more purposeful in the future so this wouldn't happen again? Margaret made a few notes:

"Leslie, please help me understand what you heard me ask for. I'm curious about the direction you heard me give in regard to this product. What I'm looking at is not what I expected to receive. I'm wondering what I may have said that contributed to the direction this product followed. How can we work together to create what I need?"

The question building block supports action and empowerment, because it comes from a place of curiosity rather than blame or judgment. Looking to the future gives both parties more space within which to create actions and solutions.

Building Block 4: Reveal

Once you have heard the other person, you can then ask to share your thinking. Generally, when people feel heard, they are more likely to extend the same courtesy to the other person in a conversation. When it is your turn, you can share your thinking and then bring the other person back into the conversation by asking them what you may be missing.

It is important to frame your messages clearly and be direct so that the other person is most likely to get it. At the same time, you will want to stay open to any new information that may come your way and be responsible for how your feelings and reactions may influence your thinking. This will help you avoid jumping to conclusions based on untested assumptions. Consider this example:

In Rob's morning team meeting, he announced that Jim would be representing their area on the modernization task force. Ellen clearly showed a negative reaction to this news, and Rob asked her to stop by his office. When Ellen came in, Rob said, "I was surprised by your reaction this morning when I announced that Jim would be representing us on the modernization task force. When we discussed that opportunity, you told me that you were buried with the new publications app and couldn't take on any new projects until January. You also said that when it came to 'modernization' you had 'been there, done that.' So, I need some help understanding your reaction."

In this circumstance, Rob explained what led to the decision he announced in the staff meeting, and he tested his interpretation of Ellen's behavior. He demonstrated an openness to new information she might provide. He also set the stage for a positive conversation in which they can both clarify their intentions, avoid assumptions, and move forward in a productive way.

Building Block 5: Challenge

Part of the process of working to a conclusion or a mutual understanding involves perspective taking. Put yourself in the other person's shoes or play devil's advocate to see other points of view. Sometimes you may disagree with other people. It is important to express your point of view and stay engaged in the conversation. Glossing over the difference or trying to force your point of view on another person is not effective and does not support a healthy relationship. Explaining your perspective directly with care, checking to see where there may be some points of agreement on which you can build, citing objective criteria to the extent they exist, asking questions to further the conversation, and working toward a solution all increase the chances that you will be able to craft a joint solution.

Challenging effectively is a skill set that takes practice, because listening to and considering another perspective may feel threatening and require a comfort level with ambiguity that many people do not have. It is also important to explain what you are doing so that others don't feel as though you are challenging their ideas for the sole purpose of doing so. Position yourself as a partner, raising questions to come up with the best solution, rather than trying to discredit others. Effectively using the skills in this building block will strengthen the relationships you have with others and enable you to authentically partner with others in pursuit of joint solutions.

Read through the following examples to see how you might use the challenge skill set more effectively.

In a meeting where you disagree with most of the points made by your colleagues: "I appreciate the perspectives you have offered and I don't want to sound as though I'm not a team player. I do want to share my concern that if we do not put forward a joint recommendation as promised, we will lose our opportunity to contribute to the final design. How can we make that happen?"

In a conversation with a peer who often takes on the role of martyr: "I wonder how else we can look at this situation? If you didn't feel that the other team is taking advantage of you, what action might you be willing to take?"

Pushing back on a due date your boss is requesting: "If I put myself in your shoes, I can see wanting to send these results forward ASAP. I am curious about the benefit of waiting for the analytics coming in on Monday and then sending our results. How might that strengthen our position?"

Explaining to a team member why delivering as agreed is important: "I have heard you say a day or two one way or the other doesn't matter more than once. I wonder how other team members react when you promise something by a certain time and then deliver it later with no explanation? What story might people tell themselves about your promises and what they are worth?"

Building Block 6: Negotiate

When you are negotiating with someone else, it is tempting to view them as the barrier to the solution or answer you want. They are too stubborn, inflexible, naïve, or selfish. If you find yourself focusing on the other people and directing a lot of energy their way, it may be time for you to consider your contribution to the situation at hand. Ask questions that help all parties focus on the future and support finding a solution. To what extent can you take parts of any ideas proposed and reconfigure them to create a solution to which everyone can commit? Consider the following examples:

> "Earlier you mentioned the importance of doing a dry run with the entire team. I agree with that. How can we make that happen before the scheduled presentation on Tuesday?"

"I have heard several concerns expressed about changing suppliers this late in the project. I haven't heard how we might get the current supplier to deliver a work product that doesn't require the amount of corrections we have been making. What ideas does everyone have?"

Negotiating requires you to look at your own contributions and a willingness to embrace both/and thinking. The challenge for you is to find common ground and build upon it.

Building Block 7: Commit

A commitment is a promise. For all parties to fulfill their promises, it is important for people to be clear on what they are expected to do or deliver and when. Don't rush to adjourn your conversation once you hear an initial agreement. Acknowledge the agreement and then take the time to clarify the actions each person will take so that you are more likely to achieve the successful end you all envision.

Build in some checkpoints or ways to touch base to ensure that everyone stays on track. Make note of the agreements made and share those notes with all parties. If anything looks as if it will get in the way of you keeping a commitment you made, inform the other parties at once and work out a contingency plan. Take promises seriously and do your best to always follow through as agreed.

This building block is often skipped and then people wonder what went wrong when things don't turn out as expected. Take the time to confirm understandings and clarify next steps. This will strengthen your credibility with others and give you a strong base on which to build next time. Consider the following example (Bianco-Mathis and Nabors 2015):

Carrie, I will draft the email reminding the team that you are the go-to person for legislative updates and you are going to start holding weekly team meetings beginning on the 4th. I'll look forward to receiving the meeting minutes within 48 hours of each meeting as we agreed. Regarding training, we've agreed to survey the customer service managers and identify key areas for development. What needs to happen first to get that moving? Who will update the team and by when can we expect the initial communication?

Putting It All Together

These skill sets come into play every time you engage in an important conversation. Use Table 2-2 to refine your techniques. These skill sets can stand alone, and they can support the C-O-A-CH model introduced in chapter 1.

Table 2-2. Techniques to Master Dialogue

Building Block	Techniques to Consider	Sample Language
Focus	» Identify intentions » Clarify beliefs » Access feelings » Determine difficulty » Rate importance » Reflect on being	» "What result do I want?" » "What do I think about this situation?" » "What is my reward for thinking this way?" » "How willing am I to change my mind?" » "How easy or difficult is this for me on a scale of 1-10?" » "What do I need to move forward?"
Listen	» Utilize whole heart and mind » Align nonverbals » Empathize » Use silence » Don't get hooked » Get to the bottom line	» "What basic message am I getting?" » "What impressions am I getting in addition?" » "I see what you mean . . ." » "It sounds like you are feeling unsupported; is that so?" » "To sum up, we are looking at . . ." » "In 20 words or fewer, what are our choices?"
Question	» Inquire into others' reasoning » Get more information » Reflect » Ask for feedback » Revisit the existing agreement	» "Help me understand . . ." » "Tell me more about . . . » "What result did you anticipate when . . ." » "How do you feel about . . ."

Table 2-2. Techniques to Master Dialogue (cont.)

Building Block	Techniques to Consider	Sample Language
Reveal	» Share your reasoning » Be direct with care » Assert » Offer ideas » Appreciate efforts	» "I am concerned about the number of errors in this report. I was expecting a final product we could send forward immediately and this isn't it. Help me understand what happened." » "I think we should continue to use the current supplier. The reason I think this is because they know our requirements, they are competitive price-wise, and they have a long-standing relationship with us. What do you think?" » "How might it work if . . .?"
Challenge	» Play devil's advocate » Tell a story » Reframe » Switch shoes » Reaffirm joint purpose » Consider pros and cons	» "How else can we look at this?" » If I put myself in your shoes, I can see myself getting very angry. You are working hard to get through all the requirements and contracting is slowing you down."
Negotiate	» Craft solutions » Connect the dots » Clarify criteria » Link ideas » Clarify contributions	» "What are the common elements in the ideas we've already discussed?" » "What would happen if . . .?" » "Earlier you mentioned the importance of including the team in the presentation, and I didn't hear you describe how that will happen. How are you planning to do that?"
Commit	» Paint a picture » Map out supporting steps » Make a request » Give or get permission to check in » Get moving » Box information	» "What will that look like?" » "Walk me through the new approach." » "How do you see that playing out?" » "What needs to happen first?" » "What actions can we take now?" » "Who owns this action? » "What is the consequence of doing nothing?"

Bianco-Mathis and Nabors (2017)

Consider the following example to see how these skills can strengthen your impact.

C-O-A-CH Conversation

Alan was hopeful as he headed into the conference room for the executive team meeting. He had only one item on the agenda: a conversation using the C-O-A-CH model to work through the team's past, present, and future contributions for the success of their new CFO. Alan was thankful that the team had been practicing the dialogue skills they were introduced to at the spring off-site meeting. They were going to need them to get their relationships on the right track so that they could deliver the results the board was expecting and not kill one another in the process.

Alan took a seat and looked around the room. John, his chief information officer, was talking to Angela, the general counsel. Marc, his chief human capital officer, was taking notes on his tablet and Renee, his chief member experience officer, joined the team with her characteristic burst of energy and a "good morning to all." Alan consulted his notes and took a centering breath.

> **Alan:** Good morning everyone. As you know, we have only one topic on our agenda. As an organization, we have lost two CFOs in the past 18 months. We are working on an aggressive timeline set by the board to successfully acquire one of two targeted companies by Q1 next year. (Current Situation) For us to meet this timeline and to ensure our overall health and success as an organization and an executive team, my goal for today is to identify how we can select the right CFO candidate for us and how we can set him or her up to succeed. (Objective) I'd like to hear from everyone before we jump in to make sure we're all on the same page.
>
> **John:** That is what I was expecting based on your email and our last meeting.
>
> **Angela:** Me, too. I just hope we can find a CFO who isn't so needy. I think we need a stronger executive search firm.
>
> **Marc:** I'm not certain that's the magic answer. Based on the feedback I got from the CFOs we lost, I think we've all contributed to the situation we're in.

Renee: I don't know if I agree with that. And, I am willing to look at the situation from more than one side. I think we all have to keep an open mind and be curious about how we might approach this differently so that we hire the right candidate this next time around.

Alan: OK then. Let's consider an ideal scenario to ease into a conversation of alternatives. In other words, what have we learned about what we need in an ideal CFO and what have we learned about how we each can help or hinder his or her work? (Alternatives)

Angela: An ideal CFO for us will be comfortable telling our story. That means she has to get up to speed quickly and be able to effectively connect with board members, investors, and staff. Sharon couldn't do that. In my experience, if you weren't a board member, she made you feel that you weren't worth her time. How do others see it?

Renee: I agree. She loved to talk about forecasts and EBITDA, but if someone had a question about expenses or needed information for a client . . . (Renee rolls her eyes and others nod their heads.)

John: I think the ideal person will want to be a member of our team. The job is more than just a title and it's more than just focusing on finance. We have to count on that person to deliver. Sharon didn't do that.

Alan: So, I'm hearing that we need someone who is a quick study, with solid skills, able to connect and tell our story to multiple audiences. The ideal person will want to be a member of our team, be willing to look beyond their own vertical, and they will take commitments seriously—whether to a board member, staff person, or one of us. How can we use this information to do a better job of hiring Sharon's replacement? What do we have to do differently this time around?

Marc: I'd like to suggest that we team up to interview the top candidates. That way we can compare what we hear with more than one person in the room.

Angela: I agree. I think we should use that behavioral interviewing approach you shared with us once. We could focus on the interpersonal stuff that caused the last two folks to fail.

Alan: How can we create an early warning system so that if we see anything not going as planned, we can step in and fix the problem immediately? In retrospect, I feel as though we let a lot of things linger with Sharon. At least I did.

Renee: Well, we could be purposeful in checking in with the new person. Not just about the work, but about how they're getting up to speed and how the interactions are going. (Alternatives)

Marc: And, we can probably be more aware of feedback from staff and others. We know some of the traps in our environment. We can be proactive and work to make sure the new person doesn't fall into them.

Angela: I think we can also compare notes. The problems that Sharon had and Paul before her were similar. Some of us were aware of some of the problems. We didn't talk to each other, so we didn't know the extent to which things were unraveling until it was too late. Maybe it was less "neediness" on Sharon's part and more "awareness" on our parts?

Alan: Good observation, Angela. So, we set up a safety net and each of us has a role in making sure the selection process for the new CFO is as strong as possible. We create a mentoring or coaching plan to set the person up for success, and we compare notes to catch and correct problems early. Does that cover it? (Choice) (Nods around the table). OK then, let's drill down a bit to clarify what these behaviors will look like and who will do what so we are all in agreement about how we are going to move forward.

In this conversation, all the dialogue building blocks were used. Alan began the meeting with a clear focus on the intended result. Members of the team agreed and disagreed with each other, and they made it clear that they were listening in both cases. They asked questions and shared their own thinking. They challenged themselves to come up with strategies that would increase their chances for success. They negotiated how they might implement those strategies. And, they committed to the process.

Making It Real

This chapter discussed the building blocks of dialogue and provided practical examples of ways in which they can be used to create and expand meaningful conversations. Consider your conversations and rank the building blocks from most used to least used.

1. Select one of the most-used building blocks and note the language you use currently. How might you build on this strength? What language might you begin to incorporate?

2. Select one of the least-used building blocks and consider how you can begin to practice in this area. What language might you begin to incorporate? With what expected result?

3. Track your progress over the next 30 days. Once you are comfortable with one building block, add another. Note the impact the new language has on your conversations and the results you experience.

PART 2:
Navigating the Seven Cs

Part 2 takes you forward on a journey following the Seven Cs Coaching Map. Each chapter introduces concrete tools you can apply immediately as you consider your own opportunities with colleagues and clients. As you read about context and purpose, assess your own circumstances. How would you describe your organization's coaching culture? What role do data play for you and how might you incorporate the information about data to strengthen your workplace? Consider the approach to planning and committing to action and identify content that can support your own work. You will find many examples demonstrating sample language and options in situations that will undoubtedly sound familiar to you. Follow the map. You will become more conversant with coaching language and you will find a wide range of substantive content as you move closer toward your destination of a coaching culture.

3

Capture Context and Clarify Purpose

As noted in previous chapters, "there is a growing movement among organizations to develop a coaching culture as more companies realize the advantages of such a strategy" (ICF 2016, 3). In theory, this means that organizations of all kinds may be jumping on the coaching bandwagon. In practice, this means that some organizations will do so successfully and others will not. The differentiating factors are found in what we call *context* and *purpose*.

Consider the case of Michael. He is the CEO of a midsize not-for-profit. He travels frequently to meet with members and stakeholders and when he does, he uses his time to catch up on business articles, TED Talks, and other content outside his immediate purview. When he returns to the office, he tasks his senior team with implementing the new ideas he has read about.

Michael is bright and well intentioned. And he is driving his staff crazy. The truth is that Michael is not open to feedback, particularly when it is personal. He is in favor of change as long as it is someone else doing the changing. His staff knows this, so when he talks about his interest in creating a coaching culture, they are skeptical. Those who have been around for a while remember what happened when they shared their thoughts as part of a 360-degree feedback initiative. It did not turn out well for some team members. What Michael says he wants and what happens when he gets it are vastly different.

Given the context within which Michael's team operates day to day, they are wondering about his purpose. What does he really want? How can they start a conversation with him to find out? What will happen if they honor his stated intention? How can they share their concerns and explore with Michael what will be different this time? Without additional clarification on context and purpose, creating a coaching culture in this organization is likely going to be an uphill battle.

Now, consider Curtis's approach to coaching. Curtis took over as director of a key office within a government agency. He inherited a culture wherein people had been punished for sharing information and providing feedback, particularly to upper management. Curtis believed in communicating with all his employees and managers, and he purposefully set about creating a culture within which people would learn those skills and be safe in practicing them. He provided training for everyone. He began a regular series of meetings with his managers and supervisors and expected them to do the same with their direct reports. He created listening sessions and shared the outputs with everyone. He helped his team identify and share metrics of success, and then he supported them in making progress and celebrating along the way.

Curtis was open to feedback and openly shared what he was working on, personally and for the office. He explained why he was doing what he was doing. He involved others in his development and the development of the office. In this office, the leader's "talk" and his "walk" were aligned. The context within which Curtis and his managers and staff operated was transparent and credible. Their intention was clear. Over a five-year period, Curtis and his team substantially transformed themselves.

Deconstructing Context and Purpose

Context describes the container in which coaching will be introduced and practiced in an organization. Purpose answers the question, "Why?" In the second example, context and a clearly defined purpose supported a coaching culture—Curtis shared his intentions and commitment, was open to feedback as a leader, proved himself to be authentic when he asked for information, shared information with managers and employees, made goals and progress discussable, and provided resources for his staff to grow and develop.

In the other example, context and purpose did not support Michael's stated intentions. He was not credible with his staff—his actions were not aligned with his stated intentions. It is unlikely that Michael's staff will fully engage in any effort that requires them to speak honestly and, in so doing, be vulnerable. History has taught them to play it safe, which is what they'll do.

To successfully build a coaching culture, consider these five elements of context and purpose: expectations, readiness, fit, agreements, and data. Let's take a closer look at each element.

Expectations

For a coaching culture to take root and grow in a healthy way, expectations must be made clear. What does the organization believe about coaching, and how knowledgeable and supportive are they of the coaching process? What biases exist within the organization and how will they help or hinder the coaching process? Will coaching be seen as a benefit or a punishment? How will leaders act in support of coaching? Who is eligible to participate in and receive the benefits of coaching, and with what intended results? What are credible measures of success within the organization? What information does the organization find credible? How will the information be gathered and shared, and with whom? Finally, how willing is the organization to let people change their behavior and see them in a new way?

These questions require answers so the organization and everyone within it knows what to expect. With answers, you can define everyone's expectations about coaching. Some are even more foundational and are linked to the leader's behavior. Michael and Curtis stated similar objectives, but their history and behavior sent a different message to their staff. Expectations have to be thought through so the context and purpose around the coaching culture is consistent, credible, and strong.

Readiness

As detailed in chapter 1, coaching is fundamentally about "unlocking people's potential" (Whitmore 2011, 10) and "making progress towards a preferred future" (Matthews 2010, 5). How do you know if an organization or an individual is ready to do the work required to achieve those outcomes? To gauge readiness for coaching, start with some "why" questions:

- Why are you considering coaching?
- Why now?

Move on to some "what" questions:

- What results do you expect to achieve through coaching?
- What work are you prepared to do to achieve those results?

And finally, wrap up with a few "how" questions:

- How willing are you to take an honest look at yourself and the contribution you are making to your current circumstances?
- How willing are you to make changes?
- How will you know when you've achieved your desired results?
- How will you be in this new space?

When considering an organization-wide change, you should be able to clearly convey the rationale for such a change, linked to expected business results and outcomes. And you should be able to paint a clear picture of the resources that will be available to support people as they move in the stated direction. As with any behavioral change, creating a coaching culture will require energy and constant practice as you work to incorporate this new way of being. The tone and speed of conversations and the language being used will be different. Some people will feel exposed. Some people will feel empowered. Some people will opt out. Despite all the benefits of coaching, not everyone is prepared to go all in. Consider these examples:

The president of a large residential construction company detailed his commitment to leadership development for himself and his top team. Part of the process required participation in an off-site leadership program and 360-degree feedback. The team agreed to support the process, and the team members scheduled their attendance in the program and then their feedback. After continually moving herself to the bottom of the schedule, the vice president of finance announced her resignation. In her exit interview, she revealed that she didn't believe in the self-reflection the process required.

Nick is an external coach working with a midsize organization. He received a call from a client indicating that she wanted to provide coaching for one of her professional staff. When he inquired about the circumstances, the client revealed that the staff member had recently engaged in some "flame mail" traffic with another colleague. The client wanted Nick to work with the staffer. "Toward what end?"

Nick asked. "What do you mean?" the client responded. Nick asked, "Has the staffer's supervisor spoken with him to convey that the behavior is unacceptable?" The client responded, "Well, no. But the staffer should know." Nick then asked, "What is the consequence for the staffer of demonstrating this behavior?" The client was thoughtful: "There really isn't a consequence per se. This staffer does great work and is on track to be promoted at the end of the month." "Sounds like you have a management opportunity, not a coaching one," Nick said.

Alicia had been working with Neil for six months. He had selected her from a pool of coaches that his organization made available for managers. He identified a set of desired results and agreed to a data-gathering process that involved having Alicia speak with colleagues, direct reports, and Neil's boss. Interestingly, they all shared a similar view of Neil's strengths and opportunities for development.

Neil heard the feedback and acknowledged that it wasn't a surprise. He committed to creating an action plan to work through the issues. He then canceled the next four coaching meetings, citing schedule conflicts, and this morning, Alicia received another email asking to reschedule. She sent an email to Neil expressing her belief that they move forward with their remaining coaching hours so that Neil can realize the benefit of the process. Neil answered saying that he doesn't want Alicia to think he hasn't gotten value from the process or his work with her. If she thinks it is important, he will have his assistant work with her to find time in his calendar. Alicia sent back a note thanking Neil for the opportunity to support him and observing that perhaps his schedule currently is too busy for coaching. She invited him to contact her in the future if he can carve out time for coaching work.

These examples demonstrate the organizational and personal nature of readiness. An organization has to be clear and realistic about what it expects from coaching and how coaching fits with other development processes. Leadership has to act in a consistent, credible fashion. Individuals have to hold themselves accountable. Coaching requires courage on everyone's part to explore strengths and consider areas to change or develop. Not everyone and not every organization is prepared to look at themselves in this way.

Fit

The extent to which an organization or an individual employee feels a connection with a particular coach can influence the quality of the work they'll do together. This connection can also be described as "fit." To assess your fit to coach another employee or a direct report, consider these variables:

- life experience
- coaching experience
- education
- style and personality
- credibility
- knowledge of the client's working environment.

In addition to this partial list of variables, you will want to ask yourself, "Am I the best coach for this person?" "Can I help this person achieve his or her goals?" You may be an excellent coach. But if the fit isn't there, you owe it to yourself and the other person to move on. Consider these examples of bad and good fit:

Ellen is an internal coach with ATI. She has worked with several managers in the company, most recently with Sam in marketing. As part of their work, Sam shared his experiences with Paul, a director in finance. These experiences, corroborated by data gathering on Ellen's part, revealed that Paul has an intriguing definition of truth and openness. Paul reached out to Ellen to explore a coaching relationship. Given what she knew about Paul, Ellen wasn't comfortable becoming his coach and suggested Paul might be better served by another coach.

Alan is an external coach who often works with C-level executives at a well-known medical society. He is known for communicating directly with care, and he has helped many clients successfully transition from a medical environment to an association environment with more of a business focus. In an initial meeting with Dr. James, he shared his outlook and coaching approach. Dr. James expressed her interest in working with Alan because she values honest communication and believes Alan will create a space within which she can explore how best to leverage her strengths and work on developing new skills.

Whether the coach is internal or external, fit is critical to consider. Coaching work requires a strong partnership, which is served by paying close attention to the coach and client fit.

Agreements

In a formal coaching relationship with an external coach, the coach and client will likely have a signed, written agreement. This agreement will outline ethical considerations such as professional conduct, conflicts of interest, the parameters of confidentiality, and logistics such as the number of meetings, notice of cancellation, and commitment to raise questions or concerns. External coaches make clear the nature and boundaries of their relationship with their client. They create the space within which the coachee is supported and invited to engage in honest conversation and exploration of issues to support expressed areas of focus for growth and development.

In a formal coaching relationship with an internal coach, the coach also makes clear the parameters of the coaching relationship so that the questions she asks and the conversation she has with her client supports the client's expressed areas of focus for growth and development. While the scope of the agreement may not be as broad as the agreement with an external coach, having a written agreement supports an internal coach in:
- punctuating the coaching relationship
- clarifying roles and responsibilities
- clearly conveying boundaries
- safeguarding confidentiality.

Often when reviewing the coaching agreement (Table 3-1) in an early meeting, the coachee may realize that he is not ready to take on the work and the responsibility that the coaching process requires. The person may have expressed an interest in coaching because he thought it was a way to "get answers" or because one or more of his peers had a coach. It is good to discover these issues early so that no one wastes anyone's time.

Table 3-1. Coaching Agreement Checklist

The Coaching Agreement
» We will hold regular coaching meetings.   » Example: We will hold meetings every two weeks beginning March 1.
» We will hold a minimum of six coaching meetings beyond the data feedback meeting.   » Example: After the data feedback meeting, we'll hold six coaching meetings by May 1.
» We will communicate outside of coaching meetings using phone and email.   » Example: Between regular face-to-face meetings, we will return each other's email and cell phone messages within 24 hours.
» We will use an agreed-upon protocol for postponing or canceling meetings.   » Example: The client and the coach will give 24 hours' notice for postponing or canceling a coaching meeting for reasons other than a personal emergency.
» We will use an action plan format for documenting actions and progress.   » Example: The client will be responsible for the agenda at each coaching meeting. The coach will document client progress at each meeting following the elements of the coaching action plan format discussed and agreed upon.
» The coaching partnership is based on mutual performance expectations.   » Example: The coach's performance expectations are to support the client in progressing toward achievement of coaching objectives in improved teamwork and organization. The client's performance expectations are to achieve measurable results as documented in the coaching plan toward improved teamwork and organization.
» The coaching partnership will measure results before and after coaching.   » Example: A 360-degree survey method will be used for pre- and post-coaching data collection to measure behavior effectiveness of the coaching objectives.
» The coach will explore desired outcomes, fears, and feelings.   » Example: The coaching conversation is a safe place for confidential dialogue. The coach will ask probing questions designed to inquire into the client's reasoning, test the client's assumptions, and surface beliefs, feelings, and ideas for action.
» The coach and client will set a protocol for handling problems.   » Example: If the client or coach perceives any issue that adversely affects the effectiveness of the coaching partnership, both parties agree to identify the issue for dialogue. If mutual dialogue does not satisfy the needs of the client and the coach, they agree that the director of human resources may be consulted for further action.
» The coaching partnership is confidential.   » Example: The coach follows the ICF ethical guidelines and provides a copy of these guidelines to the client. All coaching conversations are confidential except those conversation elements specifically agreed to by the client as not confidential.
» The client is ensured final decision making in choosing a coach.   » Example: The client is given three potential coaches to interview. The client chooses the coach determined to be the best fit.

Adapted from Bianco-Mathis, Roman, and Nabors (2008, 36)

When the coach is also the client's manager, a written agreement may not be commonly used. In this case, the manager and her employee will still want to talk through what they can expect from each other and how they might distinguish a coaching conversation from any other they might have. Some managers have found it useful to consider wearing different hats when they are coaching and using that language.

Managers have an inherent challenge in that their relationship with coachees is defined foundationally by the manager and direct report dynamic. In the role of coach, the manager will likely want to ask certain questions to spur the coachee's thinking and to encourage reflection. The manager may want to be more directive, which does not support the coaching role. To convey clear signals, it can be helpful for the manager to describe what hat she is wearing when making a given request or asking a certain question.

For example, during a coaching conversation, a manager may experience resistance on the part of the coachee. After asking several questions, the manager may say something like, "I appreciate your intention to include the other team members in the final product. Because we have a hard deadline of Friday, I need to remove my coaching hat and put on my manager's hat and ask you to move ahead with the input you already have."

If coaching language is being used in many venues, including in casual conversations between peers within the organization, a written agreement is not likely to be created. In this case, peers can still ask whether it would be helpful for them to coach before jumping into that role. Consider these examples:

As Anne and Kevin were leaving the all-staff meeting, Anne noticed that Kevin seemed to be preoccupied. During the meeting, he had also seemed to be preoccupied, which was not like him.

Anne: "What's on your mind?"

Kevin: "I've got something coming up, and I'm not sure how to handle it."

Anne: "How helpful would it be if I coach you in thinking it through?"

Kevin: "That would be great. I really need to think through some options."

When Karen and Shareefa met for their scheduled coaching meeting, Shareefa raised the following question:

Shareefa: "Before we start today, I want to share something with you."

Karen: "Of course. You know we both agreed to speak honestly and directly with each other."

Shareefa: "I know that it says so in our coaching agreement. I wasn't certain exactly how that would come into play until you shared the feedback from my team in our last meeting. You might have noticed, I wasn't too happy to hear they think I am micromanaging them. I suggested that they were wrong in what they said or that you had misunderstood. You encouraged me to think about my specific behaviors and interactions. Bottom line, you listened to me and didn't let me explain away what my staff is experiencing. You created that space that I laughed about when we went over it initially so that I could hear a tough message and think about what to do with it. I wanted to thank you for that."

Karen: "You are entirely welcome. That is part of our agreement and my commitment to you. I'm glad to hear you found it of value."

Shareefa: "For now, I wanted to acknowledge it and tell you I appreciate the 'direct with care' language you used. I'll let you know about the value."

Karen: "Fair enough."

In these examples, the individuals have a clear, shared understanding of the way they are going to speak to each other. Whether the coaching agreement is written or unwritten, individuals must agree on their roles and the process through which they will demonstrate their support.

Data

Data serve to enrich the coaching process. Initial data collection can create a baseline from which you can measure progress. Ongoing data collection can reinforce progress and provide feedback to clients on their efforts. Personal preference, experience, and what is credible for the client and the organization will influence the extent to which you can collect data. Multiple data sources can inform and enrich the coaching process. Table 3-2 notes the benefits and shortcomings of these data sources. Data will be discussed in depth in chapter 4. For now, let's consider three main sources of data:

1. the client
2. the environment
3. direct observation.

Table 3-2. Data Sources Benefits and Shortcomings

Data Source	Benefits	Shortcomings
The Client	» Easy access » Credible though limited source of information » Provides window into thinking » Coach can question data as related to stated objectives	» One point of view » Information shared through filters » Picture is likely incomplete
The Environment	» More complete information » Opportunity to bring the environment along » Demonstrates openness	» May raise conflicts or inconsistencies » Creates expectations
Direct Observation	» Coach can share information in the moment » Client can consider any gaps between intention and impact » Client can reword or rethink the approach » Coach and client can have a rich conversation with real-time data	» Requires skillful feedback » Opportunities to observe targeted behaviors may be limited

The Client

Throughout your relationship, your client is your primary source of data. Energy level, tone, pacing of speech, focus, and reactions to topics being discussed reveal the client's perspective. In addition to the content of your conversations with the client, you will have the opportunity to have the client:

- Complete self-assessments.
- Read and comment on books, articles, TED Talks, and other content.
- Keep a journal of reflections and report on lessons learned.

Because you follow the client's agenda, it makes sense to keep the client front and center regarding the information you collect and use.

The Environment

A secondary source of data is the environment. If you are an internal coach or the client's manager, you will have ongoing access to people who interact with the client, such as other staff, customers, suppliers, and members. If you are an external coach, you may have an opportunity to:

- Interview colleagues and others.
- Read performance appraisals.
- Review sales, service, or performance data.

You may find that information has been shared honestly with your client; sometimes, that is not the case. Creating a credible source of feedback and clear, agreed-upon measures of success sets your client up for a positive outcome. If the client agrees to involve his environment, employees can demonstrate their openness to feedback and the coaching process by inviting others to share their thinking. If they choose to do so, they can then go back to those participants and divulge what they are working on and ask for periodic feedback about their progress. Being open about work in progress demonstrates a strength and willingness to hear and act on feedback. The effect is to "bring the environment" along in viewing the client in a new way. No matter what individuals think about someone, when they are asked to participate in this process, they invariably respect the courage being demonstrated by the person in soliciting this information.

Direct Observation

At a minimum, you will be able to consider your client's behavior when you are meeting. If you are meeting in person (or through Zoom or Skype), the client's body language and all nonverbal cues provide a substantial source of information. You will experience in real time what your client says and does, how she processes information, and how she comes to conclusions, and you will be able to observe these behaviors and ask questions to help her consider her thinking and impact. Consider this example:

> Marla invited Jack to attend her staff meeting so that he could provide her with some feedback. When Jack attended Marla's staff meeting, he saw her interact with her team in a purposeful, direct, supportive way. She had prepared an agenda with their input and distributed it in advance. Marla began the meeting by asking managers to provide an update on their key projects. They did so, and Jack noticed they weren't afraid to note problems they were encountering or to solicit ideas from their peers. The other managers shared their thoughts without hesitation and together they worked through challenges. Marla stepped in only once when they got stuck and agreed to pursue a piece of information from a peer when he asked her to do so. The team was focused on their agenda and still managed to joke with one another and laugh about their upcoming holiday plans. Their energy level was contagious, and when Jack left the meeting 90 minutes later (as scheduled), he felt great.

> Later Jack shared his observations with Marla: what she did, what she said, her team's reactions, and his perceptions of their interactions. Jack asked Marla if she would do the same for him at his next staff meeting.

Creating and Holding the Space

In addition to the elements of context and purpose noted in this chapter (expectations, readiness, fit, agreements, and data), there is one additional element that has a powerful impact on any coaching experience: the way you view yourself and others has a tremendous impact on your effectiveness as a coach. This is true whether you are an external or internal practitioner, a manager coaching an employee, or a peer coaching a peer. Before your first coaching conversation, you have to be clear about your beliefs in regard to coaching and what you intend to accomplish. As referenced in chapter 1, who you are affects your language and your conversations with others. Your mindset is foundational in creating an effective coaching space.

Case Study

With some background on the importance of capturing context and clarifying purpose when embarking on a coaching relationship, let's introduce Julie and Bob, whom we'll track through the Seven Cs Coaching Map. This case illustrates techniques and tools that can be used in different coaching situations—formal, informal, peer to peer, boss to direct reports, colleague to colleague—and any other coaching situation that flourishes in a coaching organization.

Julie is president and CEO of a high-tech company, Leading Edge. Even though she has only been a CEO for two years, Julie is a very effective leader with natural talent. She is very well liked and respected by staff and all members of her leadership team. Members of the board see her as effective and results-oriented. Unfortunately, there is one board member, Matt—the one who also owns the most stock in the company—who is very difficult to work with, tends to yell at and criticize Julie at board meetings, and is never satisfied with how the company is doing. Julie decided to work with an outside coach to address her relationship with the difficult owner and to hone her skills in a couple of other areas she wants to master. In the past few months she chose, met, and began a coaching relationship with a seasoned and professional coach, Bob.

Bob is a former executive who spent most his career building and selling three successful software startups. He credits his success to his ability to recognize and leverage individual and team talent. This influenced him to become a credentialed coach and to work with his former peer group—other CEOs. Bob is able to provide solid coaching and knowledge of the industry and the challenges his clients face. His powerful questions and calm style allow him to stimulate his clients' thinking and help them reach new levels of insight, awareness, and results.

Julie shared her expectations during the interviewing process. She was open about her current challenges and her readiness to work on herself. She felt a connection and fit with Bob and is confident that he will support and challenge her to grow as a person and as a leader. The coaching agreement she and Bob signed outlined the logistics of the coaching relationship and detailed how they will work together, what they can count on from each other, how they will handle questions and concerns should they come up, and how they will measure and track progress. Julie also considered a number of options Bob presented regarding data and how to best involve her environment. Read on to chapter 4 to find out how Julie and Bob progress through their coaching journey.

Making It Real

In this chapter, we reviewed the elements of context and explored their impact on a successful coaching experience. Think about your organization (or a client organization) and consider the following questions:

1. What is your organization's perception of coaching?
2. How credible will employees find an effort to create a coaching culture?
3. How would you rate your organization's readiness for coaching?
4. How might you introduce coaching into your organization?
5. In looking for external coaches, what aspects of "fit" will be most important?
6. What types of data will be most credible for employees and managers in your organization?

4

Collect and Feed Back Data

Once the coachee articulates her purpose for wanting to be coached, she will have a conversation with her coach wherein she will identify what realizing that intended result will look like. What will be different? How will she know? How will she measure her progress? Data support the coaching process and enable a coachee to track her progress throughout her coaching journey. This chapter closely reviews components of collecting and feeding back data, with focus on multiple ways to collect data, phases of sorting and analyzing themes, techniques for sharing data with coachees, and the important step of inviting others to observe and give additional feedback to the coachee. This chapter also addresses the "feedback mindset," which requires courage on the part of both the coach and coachee.

Let's explore and review a set of concepts and techniques you can use in your own practice as you move from gathering data, providing feedback, developing action plans, and supporting coachees toward delivering results. Although these steps are shared in a linear fashion, it is important to remember that dialogue and following the Seven Cs Coaching Map are not necessarily a lock-step process. They ebb and flow, sometimes requiring a return to further refine the purpose or revisit the data when developing a goal or assessing progress. The models and steps provide guideposts to keep you centered. All steps should be covered, but can be revisited and repeated as needed.

Gathering Data

Data are used throughout coaching to give meaningful feedback. Through feedback, the coachee learns about himself and impact of his behaviors. This encourages reflection and promotes testing of various perspectives. Data are gathered, collated, and reviewed to help coachees zero in on the purpose of engaging in a coaching process and then again when developing goals, formulating action steps, and assessing progress. Data concerning strengths and areas to grow can come from the coachee's personal reflections or through surveys, interviews, focus groups, and observations. They can be delivered formally or dropped in a passing conversation. Data help to align intentions with perceptions. They provide the basis for comparing where you are to where you want to be.

Studying and reflecting on feedback encourages individuals and teams to demonstrate openness and accountability and identify their own cognitive dissonance. If you consider yourself to be a good problem solver and rate yourself a 5 out of 5, but your peers rate you a 2.5, then there needs to be a discussion to determine why the scores are different. If an organization believes it is delivering exemplary customer service and recent customer surveys verify that notion, the organization knows to continue on course and reinforce existing practices.

In their book *Thanks for the Feedback,* Douglas Stone and Sheila Heen (2014) point out that there are three forms of feedback data: appreciative, evaluative, and coaching. In the world of work, we know that a boss can thank an employee for completing an important report ahead of schedule, evaluate an employee on certain competencies during a performance appraisal, or discuss an employee's progress toward demonstrating greater teamwork over six months of coaching meetings. It is important to remember these three distinctions. Coaching should be developmental, not judgmental. Both coach and coachee need to review data with an eye toward a future scenario. And although coaches and coachees can certainly express appreciation of one another, the process is based on holding the coachee's agenda, keeping him accountable, highlighting choices, and mutually developing pathways to goals that are important to him.

As with so much within the field of coaching, collecting and feeding back data includes both technical and interpersonal components. Let's first address the more technical elements of data gathering and analysis, and then move to the cognitive aspects of sharing the data.

Data Collection and Tools

When working with a coachee—formally or informally, up, down, or side-ways—there are three sources from which to collect data:

- the coachee's external contacts: clients, customers, suppliers, and others the coachee works with who reside outside the organization
- the coachee's internal colleagues: co-workers, "inside" customers, bosses, and direct reports
- the coachee: the coachee's own self-reports or what you, the coach, observe from interacting with the coachee.

These sources are relevant whether the coachee is an individual, team, or an entire organization. What do members of a leadership group claim to be the strength of the entire team? What do customers say about an entire organization? How do employees view middle management? What behaviors does a CEO personally believe she needs to practice to be more effective? And even more insightful, what do you experience as the coach interacting with the coachee in the moment?

Choosing a data collection method or tool depends on what best supports the coachee. You weigh the pros and cons of each method and concentrate on the desired results. Once information is gathered, it needs to be sorted into meaningful themes that are most likely to be heard and understood by the receiver. Information is powerful when it is used to seek continuous improvement.

There are essentially seven data collection methods commonly used by practitioners: self-assessment inventories, 360-degree surveys, climate and employee opinion surveys, focus groups, image studies, individual and group observation, and one-on-one feedback. They are described as follows:

- **Self-assessment inventories** can be used by individuals or teams to assess personality, style, values, career skills, or management competencies. Examples include Myers-Briggs Type Indicator, Emotional Intelligence Inventory, Thomas-Kilmann Conflict Mode Instrument, and Career Architect. Such instruments tend to be easy and quick to use. It is best to use self-assessment in combination with other data-gathering methods to ensure balance and multiple perspectives.

- **360-degree surveys** can be administered online and completed by the coachee and the coachee's superiors, colleagues, peers, direct reports, and customers. They can be designed for individuals or teams, and are based on competencies such as leadership, emotional intelligence, or other tailored skill sets. Examples include BarOn Emotional Quotient Inventory, Suite of 360 Assessments (from the Center for Creative Leadership), Hogan Assessments, and FeedbackPlus. These inventories are valid and reliable, provide both statistical and narrative data, and usually include templates for action planning. Results are provided by those who interact with the coachee regularly and provide a gap analysis between the coachee's view and the view of others. Results are composite and confidentiality is ensured. On the other hand, they can be costly and may require specific training on the part of the coach.
- **Climate and employee opinion surveys** can be off-the-shelf or tailored and delivered to entire divisions or organizations to measure the level of satisfaction around specified organizational dimensions (decision making, career development, culture, benefits). Examples include SurveyMonkey, DecisionWise, and Hay Group Surveys. These surveys are valid and reliable and can be valuable for organization-wide planning and continuous improvement. However, they can be costly and take time to administer.
- **Focus groups** are facilitated sessions with people across an organization, with discussion on topics concerning one specific group or the entire organization. Data are gathered on flipcharts by a notetaker or electronically. The information is collated into themes without attribution. Results are qualitative and the process requires trained facilitators and researchers.
- **Image studies** require a trained coach with expertise in sorting through personal and face-to-face qualitative data. The process is similar to a 360-degree assessment, but the data are gathered directly by the coach, who interviews the coachee and the coachee's superiors, direct reports, peers, and customers. The questions and process are designed by a trained coach, who collates the data into themes and presents the data to the coachee during a coaching session. The benefit of this

technique is the rich data obtained, which in turn leads to more meaningful understanding and action planning.

- **Individual and group observation** occurs when the coach accompanies and observes the coachee going about work activities, interacting with others, attending meetings, and so on. The data are gathered in real time and provide immediate behavior assessment.
- **One-on-one feedback** refers to a person (coach, colleague, boss, direct report) who experiences another person exhibiting a certain behavior and decides to give direct feedback to that person. For example, a colleague may decide to give feedback to one of his officemates who keeps interrupting conversations. Another example would be when a coach notes that her coachee keeps blaming others during coaching meetings. It would be useful for the coach to make an observation that will help the coachee realize that he's blaming others.

As you can see, each method comes with pros and cons. For example, conducting effective focus groups takes expertise and training, the use of certain inventories requires certification, and image studies require time and a high level of trust. Additionally, choosing which method or combination of methods to use depends on a number of factors: time, cost, number of participants, confidentiality, acceptance level of the coachee, and ultimate use of the data. The analysis questions provided in Table 4-1 are useful in contemplating the most appropriate approach.

Table 4-1. Choosing Data Collection Methods

Consideration	Questions to Ask
Best Fit	» What data will the client and the client's environment find credible? » Are the data narrative or statistical? » What tool will best support their learning style and culture? » What will best support the intended results of the coaching?
Available Resources	» How much time is available for data gathering and analysis? » What is the budget? » How much time are raters willing and able to spend? » What will provide the best depth and breadth?

Table 4-1. Choosing Data Collection Methods (cont.)

Consideration	Questions to Ask
Intended Use of Data	» What will provide the best data that will move the client to action? » What is the level of interest in raters participating again for a follow-up? » How important is both pre- and post-coaching data? » What is the need to offer both individual and team or entire company results?

The advantages of carefully choosing the right data-gathering tools can mean the difference between acceptance and rejection of the feedback. If a director of marketing has been told that she is vindictive when someone criticizes her, it would be prudent to choose a data-gathering method that provides confidentiality, such as a 360-degree assessment. A survey would be best if an executive team believes that only one customer is disgruntled, when in fact multiple customers are displeased with the company's service. A survey can indicate that four out of five customers rated the company poorly, and the executive team would have to face that reality.

Data Analysis

As you collect data as a coach, you will be creating notes, files, spreadsheets, and charts of information in myriad formats. How do you make sense of it all? And more important, how do you organize the data into a format that will assist the coachee in processing the feedback and moving to action?

Sorting feedback data and into manageable themes is like writing a research paper. Let's say you are writing a paper on corporate sustainability. As you conduct research, read books and articles, watch a few videos, and peruse newspaper clippings, you begin to sort the information into related topics—definition of corporate sustainability, different types, importance to the organization, specific examples from major organizations, typical challenges and how to plan for them, associated costs, how to implement and gain buy-in, and how to measure and track results. There is no "right" or "wrong" with these categories; rather, they resonate with you and the kind of paper you want to write given your audience, purpose, and desired reactions.

The same is true when organizing coaching data. Two different coaches may consolidate the data using variant headings and frames. The point is not that all the categories are the same; rather, the intent is to develop headings and homogenize the information into chunks that the coachee can consider, embrace, or reject. Chunking allows questioning, reflection, and real learning, whereas vast quantities of random information can cause confusion and immobility.

Just as you would find in the research on corporate sustainability, the data concerning a particular coachee may be inconsistent. The only way to reconcile such differences is to dig into the data in more depth. You can expand your data collection and add more interviews or conduct an additional focus group. Additionally, with your coachee, you can ask clarifying questions, analyze the data under different circumstances, and discern the reasoning behind some of the opposing data points.

For example, let's say a coachee gets feedback from her 360-degree inventory that her presentations are strong. Yet, at the same time, feedback from interviews with her peers indicates that her presentation skills are weak. Based on the face value of this input, her coach might guide her toward watching a video on how to make presentations interesting and organized. Yet, in reality, it turns out that the coachee's problem is not in designing good presentations, but that she gets nervous presenting in front of groups—and that this fear holds her back not only with formal presentations, but also with participating in groups. Getting to the true meaning of a piece of data assists the coachee in pinpointing and verbalizing her real goal.

Depending on the amount of data you are trying to manage, you can use simple sorting tools such as sticky notes and your own personally designed charts, or you can use more sophisticated tools such as spreadsheets or software packages. Again, the result is the same—organize similar data into manageable chunks. At this point, you will spend hours or even days sorting and resorting the categories and wording of the data.

A useful technique is to start with the raw data, progress to overall strengths and weaknesses, and eventually end with actual topic areas. The term *homogenized* is used because the coach condensed similar statements into one to represent a particular sentiment or issue. There are no rules other than presenting the data truthfully. The important element is that you use your method consistently and you clearly explain your method to the coachee. This is essential whether the coachee is an individual, a team, or an entire organization.

By separating the homogenized raw data into strengths and areas to develop, you can begin to see patterns in how the coachee is perceived and the results of her behaviors. These valuable insights then naturally lead into meaningful themes and topics. You can use them to confirm or reject working themes you might already have in mind during the initial data-gathering process. Yet, as you continue to collate the data, you further refine those categories through the process of sorting and resorting.

Finally, you can gather the data into manageable chunks, complete with strengths and development areas, and further supported by hypothesis statements that can be tested during dialogue and reflection with the coachee. The hypothesis statements are possible reasons—garnered from the data so far—for why the coachee behaves in certain ways. These proposed reasons provide a basis for questioning as you help the coachee peel back the layers behind her beliefs.

The benefits of sorting data thematically include:
- assisting in prioritizing action
- making it easier to formulate goals and future pictures within an action plan
- eliminating redundancy
- preventing coachees from arguing away a certain point.

As you work with your coachee's data, allow your thinking to diverge as you consider alternative perspectives and rationale. Keep asking yourself questions as you frame and reframe. Search for linkages and relationships between different data points. This will help you plan for the feedback meeting. For example, you can ask:
- How are people reacting to you?
- What behaviors are supporting you?
- What behaviors are getting in the way?
- Why did you decide to approach various situations the way you did?
- What led to the choices you made?
- What results do you want to experience?
- What has to change for you to get the results you desire?

As the coachee responds to these and other questions, it is likely that she will reveal her thinking and underlying beliefs. With this information, you can help her consider alternative beliefs and play out what behaviors would support them. The emphasis should be future focused. It is important to support the coachee in connecting the dots along the continuum of beliefs, behaviors, and results. In doing this, you can support her in developing critical thinking and the skills needed to analyze the links and discover new behaviors and results.

Feeding Back Data

Reviewing the data with the coachee supports reflection and prevents her from jumping to all-or-nothing conclusions. You can encourage her to view the data as a whole, note connections, and decide on the most beneficial areas to work. You should aim to always give the coachee the straight story and ask critical thinking questions that encourage varying views. Questions you can ask include (Bianco-Mathis, Roman, and Nabors 2008):

- What does this feedback mean to you?
- How do you feel about it?
- What are your choices?
- How do they serve you?
- What are the consequences of those choices?
- How do you move forward?
- What results do you want to achieve?
- How does this (behavior and performance) support your purpose?
- What can you do differently?
- What are the consequences of doing nothing?

In the end, coaches are effective at feeding back data when they:

- Place data in context.
- Support reflection.
- Help their clients make new connections.
- Help their clients make informed choices.

Data Gathering and Feedback Mindset

As you review the charts, tools, and approach of gathering and feeding back data, you might be feeling some pressure and even trepidation about gathering data, maintaining confidentiality, using dialogue to reveal reasoning, questioning underlying beliefs, or presenting data in a thoughtful way. Basically, whether you are the coach or the coachee, working with feedback takes courage. Think of a time when you were given feedback. Was it done well or poorly? Even if it was done well, how did you feel? Let's face it, coaching is not for lightweights. But by refining your dialogue and skills, you can stand ready for the challenge.

The coach needs courage in establishing trust, asking others to give honest feedback concerning a fellow colleague or boss, maintaining confidentiality, presenting data in meaningful chunks, and reporting data with care. In turn, a coachee must be courageous in honestly assessing herself, openly listening and processing feedback from others, prioritizing areas to work, disclosing that she is trying out new behaviors, and being willing to gather follow-up data. Both coaches and coachees are opening themselves up to scrutiny and vulnerability. Coaches need to take care of themselves, prepare diligently, hone their skills, share stories with other coaches, and accept who they are—with their own strengths and weaknesses—as they reach out to coach others. Sometimes coaches must also guide coachees through raw experiences in such a way that they not only come out stronger, but are perceived by others as being stronger.

That's a powerful challenge for all involved. Brené Brown talks about embracing vulnerability and reaching out to others as a way to be authentic, accepting the worthiness of self and connecting with the humanity in others. This requires that we be courageous, let go of the perception of who we think we need to be, and accept who we are. By doing this, we are then open to personal change and growth; the kind that takes place in coaching.

Perhaps the most effective tool for navigating this vulnerability is dialogue. A coach uses dialogue to engage coachees; in turn, coachees use dialogue within their immediate environment and throughout the organization. As explained in previous chapters, the use of dialogue techniques promotes reasoning and helps to translate emotions into meaningful expression. This makes it easier to tackle uncomfortable or sticky conversations. Armed with dialogue, coachees can more confidently reach out and take on situations that they otherwise might ignore, bury, or escape from.

It is useful to make vulnerability and courage points of discussion during the coaching process. By so doing, the coachee gains strength and confidence. Fear dissipates with practice, staying present, preparing for difficult conversations, and fiercely focusing on the "other." A coaching mantra for both coaches and coachees is to lean into the discomfort.

Best Feedback Dialogue Techniques

Chapter 2 covered dialogue in depth and shared many powerful techniques. Learning and practicing each technique is necessary to hardwire your brain. Equally important is being able to in a matter of seconds pull out just the right dialogue tool for the right situation.

In the process of giving feedback, some situations are more prevalent than others. For example, a coachee may state, "There is a mistake. This feedback is not for me. It belongs to someone else." Obviously, this represents some cognitive dissonance. How do you, as the coach, handle this with care? Initially, it is important to make sure the coachee truly has the right information. Administrative snafus happen, and your preparation and mindfulness is necessary to prevent upsetting anyone.

If the feedback is correct, first establish context and help the coachee face reality, as difficult as that may be. It is best to do this even before the coachee sees the feedback data. Then show the data and set the context picture again. Reinforcement may be needed several times. Consider this script:

> Peter, I realize this information is difficult to absorb. Reacting in a variety of ways—even disbelief—is common. I want to remind you of two things. First, if you remember [remind coachee of previous discussions], these data were collected within the context of helping you become a more effective leader. This is something you said you wanted [revisit commitment]. Although we say we want feedback, it is sometimes difficult to embrace and make decisions about what might require action. As you can see, this entire top section of your feedback report lists your strengths and the many ways in which your followers admire you and believe you are doing well [establish the balance that you have ensured exists in the data]. So, I encourage you [offer, don't demand] to keep a balanced perspective. Keep in mind that you have an entire repertoire of strengths to build on. Second, remember the previous discussion we had about perceptions versus intention? You and I need to work through these data and determine how others are experiencing you. How are others' perceptions aligned or different from your intentions? Then we can see how to use this information in service to the goals you established. Perhaps you can remind me of how you want to be experienced as a leader? [Use a question that encourages the coachee to envision moving forward.]

From here, as you and the coachee move through the data and begin to prioritize areas to work on, you will rely on your dialogue skills—and the basic infrastructure of inquiry and advocacy—to support the coachee in his exploration of the feedback. Reinforcing some of the dialogue tools covered in chapter 2, the techniques and scenarios in Table 4-2 highlight common feedback situations. Remember, no matter what method you use, it is important to bring the coachee back into the conversation through an action-oriented, thinking question.

Table 4-2. Feedback Scenarios and Techniques

Situation	Dialogue Technique
Put myself in your shoes and reframe	If I put myself in your shoes, I can understand how you might feel puzzled about this feedback. Your managers feel that you are a good presenter, yet your colleagues believe you are not a strong communicator. What are some reasons for this?
Right or wrong	I want to remind you that there is no right or wrong in these data. This information represents a point in time, and we need to consider what is being said, the validity, the reasoning behind why it might have been shared, and the options you have for accepting it or not. That said, even if your perception is different from what is being shared—or even if we have information that indicates the data are wrong and biased—there may still be action you want to take. When reviewing the data, how might keeping this mindset be helpful in your interpretation?
Reframe	That certainly is one way of interpreting that statement about your management style. Can you think of another inference you can make—something else the statement might be saying?
Give an example or story	How might your tendency to declare everything a priority cause your team to start ignoring your sense of urgency? It's like that fable of Chicken Little running around saying the sky is falling until folks stopped listening to him—and then, of course, the sky fell one day and no one was prepared. How does this inform your thinking about how to handle this feedback?
Patterns or trend	When you review the data under the decision-making theme, what patterns do you find concerning your approach as noted by both your colleagues and direct reports?

Situation	Dialogue Technique
Behaviors or results	I can understand your frustration. These are high-level people and your expectation is that they should professionally step up and take accountability. Thus, you feel resentful about having to spend time outlining the outputs you are looking for and so you don't take the time to do it. Given the data, what is the result of you not stipulating specific outcomes— and what is the implication for an alternative behavior you might think about trying?

Getting Support From Others

In our experience as coaches, we often found ourselves frustrated. For example, we would spend months coaching a leader who had decided on a future picture of more participative decision making or improved communications. The leader would practice field assignments and report on successful examples of trying out new behaviors and results. We would even spend a day observing the leader and seeing for ourselves the change over time. The frustration often came six months later in conducting follow-up interviews. We would get comments such as, "Oh, I guess Joe is doing better. I have noticed a few changes. But only yesterday he announced a decision without asking for our input. Let's face it. Joe will always be Joe." What happened here?

What happened was human nature. We all make judgments of other people. We slot them into categories in our brains: Charlie is the guy who can't stop talking; Lisa is the accountant who never smiles; Franco is a great visionary but can't find his way out of a paper bag. We do this to order our environment and make it easier to remember people. Our brains like to categorize and label. When someone comes walking down the hall, it's as if he has several labels sticking to his clothes—smart, obnoxious, sensitive, helpful, good with numbers, great communicator—all reflective of how he is perceived by others. And not only does our brain label; it likes to hold on to those labels and will then keep looking for behaviors to reinforce the already established label. This human characteristic makes it difficult when a coachee practices and starts exhibiting new behaviors.

For example, let's say our leader, Joe, starts to ask for input before making a final decision. Let's say he does this eight times out of 10. As a coach, you would acknowledge this as progress toward goal achievement. As an observer in Joe's environment—someone who has had to live with him making decision after decision without any input—you would be inclined to ignore the eight times of new behavior and only remember the two times of old behavior, because to actually see and accept the new behavior you would have to change the ingrained label in your brain. The brain would prefer not to do that.

And so we have a coaching dilemma. Sometimes the environment won't let the person change!

Collecting data, whether done by the coach or coachee, is a coaching component that "brings the environment along." To further anchor this environmental partnership, the coachee should be encouraged to thank those who provide feedback. The coachee's response to this might be, "What! Why do I have to do that? I don't feel comfortable doing that." Because of feelings of discomfort, embarrassment, or even time commitment, it is wise for the coach to emphasize the reasoning behind this activity and raise the coachee's confidence in making this happen. This usually involves some role-playing and reinforcement.

If the coachee is the one collecting the feedback, she can thank the person in the moment: "Thank you for taking the time to talk to me. Your insights are important to me and I really appreciate it." If the feedback was given through a 360-degree inventory, focus group, or third-person interview, then the coachee should have a conversation (in person or virtually) with each person and say something like this:

> Thank you for participating in giving feedback in support of my
> leadership development. As you know I'm working with an executive
> coach toward continuous improvement and I'm looking forward to
> developing some goals and adding some additional tools to my work.
> I have been given only composite data and overall themes. Given that
> I do know that I want to work on being more participative in my deci-
> sion making and sharing more information with our team. So thank
> you, and I may come to you again as I continue my leadership journey.

Now, what does this do? Basically, it alerts the environment that the coachee is:
- taking the process seriously
- going to be taking action, specifically in the two areas mentioned

- coming back for more input
- asking colleagues and others to be part of the process
- setting the expectation that new behaviors should be noticed
- demonstrating both vulnerability and personal strength—it takes integrity and authenticity to do this.

In essence, the coachee is bringing the environment along on the journey of development. The coachee is also role-modeling an exemplary way for how the process of giving and receiving feedback should be managed in the organization. When enough leaders, managers, and staff role-model this behavior, the entire culture begins to change.

Help the coachee realize that saying thank you has advantages and is a step in ensuring that her coaching work can grow and be nurtured by others—as opposed to being ignored. Asking for and thanking others for feedback early in the coaching process is one way to build support in the environment. We discuss a second method to "bring the environment along" in chapter 6.

Case Study

With the context for coaching established, Julie is now ready to review the feedback she received from her coach and prepare for her next coaching session. With her consent, Bob collected feedback on Julie using the following methods and tools:

- initial data-gathering meeting with Julie—her assessment of self

- 360-degree inventory from 12 board members and the 10 members of her leadership team

- one-on-one interviews with six members of Julie's leadership team and four of her outside advisers.

During the interviews, Bob used a very basic interview protocol: What should Julie continue to do? What should she do more of? What should she do less of? Of course, he drilled down with follow-up questions to get specific examples and behaviors. Bob also carefully questioned the interviewees on how they related to Julie and how they supported and challenged her in the areas discussed. Bob knew that such information would be helpful in guiding Julie toward involving her entire environment in the coaching process.

Julie was open to having this level of data collection because she is a believer in openness, honesty, and feedback. She is passionate about her work and wants to continuously improve. She also understands that growth comes through feedback. Over the years, Julie has learned that it is one thing to have a sense of how you are being perceived, but quite another to hear how others perceive you. Bob collated the results from all three data set findings into major themes that emerged from his analysis. This provided Julie and her coach a rich foundation of data that could be further enhanced by Julie reaching out to others during the coaching process and Bob's own observations as he coaches Julie on a regular basis.

Having gathered data on Julie, Bob progressed from the raw data to overall strengths and weaknesses to actual topic areas. He used homogenized data to boil down what her colleagues said about her into one easy to follow document. Note in Table 4-3 in the comments from interviews column the statement, "She is a great strategist. (6)." This indicates that six people said something about Julie being a great strategist. Bob used this method to indicate the strength of the statement (6) and collapsed the exact words of six different people into this one phrase. Or, perhaps one person used this exact phrase and Bob chose it as representative of the five other people.

Table 4-3. Sample of Julie's Homogenized Raw Data

Data Source	Data
Self-assessment	» I use a participative style of leadership.
	» Members of my leadership team confide that I take too long to make decisions, and I agree. I don't want to be wrong and I like to get everyone's input.
	» I need help in dealing with a very difficult board member who is abusive and attacking when talking to me in private and at meetings. Yes, he does this with everyone, but I want to be stronger in how I stand up to him.
	» I give updates and communicate often.
	» As a whole, we are meeting all our numbers and goals.
	» Some members of my team don't meet goals; they either act upon the wrong goals or take too long to deliver.
	» I believe I have the right people on my team.
	» I love my work; I'm passionate about it. I'm a good motivator.
	» I seem to be spending too much time on staff and people issues. I want to get to the exciting stuff—growing the company.

Data Source	Data
360-degree feedback	» Decisiveness is rated low by both self and others. » All board members except one rate her high on overall leadership and results. » Direct reports rate her low on delegating and setting clear expectations. » Direct reports rate her high on overall leadership, participation, and enthusiasm. » Board and direct reports believe she should spend more time in growing the company. » Direct reports rate her low and not timely in confronting and managing difficult situations and people.
Comments from interviews	» Julie is fantastic to work for. (10) » She can be trusted. She is open and honest. (10) » She takes too long to make decisions. Not every decision has to be a consensus. (7) » She is a great strategist. (6) » She needs to realize that she can make decisions and then handle things if the decision is wrong. (5) » She has very strong communication skills, written and verbal. (10) » She has to delegate more. She is involved in too many details and should be out dealing more with clients and expanding the company. (7) » She seems uncomfortable confronting difficult situations, such as pushing back on a difficult board member, facilitating a disagreement, or firing an ineffective supplier. (7)

Bob then separated strengths and areas to develop (Table 4-4). With this breakdown, he can begin to see patterns in how Julie is perceived and the results of her behaviors. For example, Julie is a strong communicator except when it comes to managing difficult situations. Bob might ask himself, "How can I help Julie transfer her communication strength to manage uncomfortable situations?" Or, Bob can more clearly note that it is not just that Julie doesn't delegate enough, but that she is also unclear in setting expectations with direct reports. These valuable insights then naturally lead into meaningful themes and topics. Bob most likely had some working themes he already used during the initial data-gathering process. Yet, as he continued to collate the data, he further refined those categories through the process of sorting and resorting.

Table 4-4. Sample Preliminary Sort of Julie's Data

What Julie Does Well	What Julie Could Do Better
Self-Assessment	
» Strong and frequent communicator » Passionate motivator » Participative style » Gets results	» Confront one difficult board member » Make more timely decisions » Guide more goal-oriented performance of direct reports » Spend more time on company growth and less time on people issues
360-Degree Feedback	
» Strong leadership characteristics » Results-oriented » Participative » Enthusiastic	» Confront difficult situations » Make more timely decisions » Delegate more with clear expectations » Grow company
Comments From Interviews	
» Well liked as a successful leader » Strong communication skills » Open and honest » Can be trusted » Strong strategist	» Confront difficult situations with board member and other internal situations » Make more timely decisions » Delegate more with clear expectations » Grow company » More openly share opinion during participative discussions

Finally, Bob did a secondary sort of Julie's data (Table 4-5). He organized the data in four manageable chunks, complete with strengths and development areas, and further supported by multiple hypothesis statements that can be tested during dialogue and reflection with Julie. As can be seen in the table, one possible conclusion is that Julie takes too much time making decisions because she fears making a mistake, doesn't have confidence in her own decisions, and believes that participation is the only way to problem solve. These proposed reasons provide a basis for questioning as Bob helps Julie peel back the layers behind her beliefs.

Table 4-5. Sample Secondary Sort of Julie's Data

Themes and Hypotheses	Strengths	Areas to Develop
Decision Making		
» Wants to make the right decisions » Wants to get everyone involved in decisions » Hesitates to make decisions; seems risk averse » Spends too much time reaching decisions » Participative style prevents her from sharing her thoughts	» Includes others in decision making, which fosters buy-in » Wants decisions to be thoughtful and right » Utilizes a participative style for increased data input and information	» Make decisions in a timely fashion; not all decisions need to be participative » Share your opinion in the participative decision-making process » Have more faith in your insights and ability to make things work, no matter the decision. » Embrace your leadership when making decisions » Utilize your strong communication skills when being clear on the purpose, timeliness, and ownership of decisions
Delegation		
» Strong communication skills » Passionate and enthusiastic » Practicing delegation would develop the leadership team » Clarifying goals and objectives of each leader can improve more focused results	» Passionate, enthusiastic, and motivating style encourages others to follow and do well » Communicates frequently with groups and individuals » Spends time on staff activities » Pays attention to details	» Would benefit from using strong communication skills in delegating and clarifying goals and expectations » Improved delegation can allow time for more CEO activities and grow leadership bench strength
Growing Company		
» Strong overall results » Viewed successful by most board members and staff » More time with clients would grow the company further	» Positively viewed by board and staff for achieving positive company results	» Improvement of delegation skills would result in more time for growth outreach » Develop and implement a plan for growing the company more diligently

Table 4-5. Sample Secondary Sort of Julie's Data (cont.)

Themes and Hypotheses	Strengths	Areas to Develop
Managing Difficult People and Situations		
» By using her strong communication skills, Julie can practice and gain confidence in managing difficult people and situations	» Strong communication skills » Preferred style is inclusion and participation	» Utilize strong communication and participative style to confront difficult people and situations » Gain confidence in managing difficult people and situations » Develop and role-play dialogue techniques for confronting the difficult board member (and other conflicts)

As she was reviewing her feedback, Julie found herself discounting the "good comments" and only concentrating on the "areas to develop." Although she was well aware that she needed to get better at decision making and confronting difficult situations, she had to admit that she was surprised at the intensity of some of the feedback. One statement at the end of the 360-degree inventory said, "Julie causes frustration when she drags her feet in making decisions concerning major issues such as structure or new products. This hesitation is hurting the company and is not indicative of a strong leader." That hit Julie hard. Her first reaction was that this was exaggerated and should be rejected. Yet Bob was very good at probing to help her see the comment from multiple perspectives.

Although Bob held up a mirror and forced Julie to look, Julie knew that Bob was in her corner no matter what the data said. Bob seemed to view each piece of data with curiosity. He never judged. He would observe and then question Julie's intentions. Bob had a way of encouraging Julie to think about choices and consequences. For example, he asked, "What is your intention when you take weeks to make a decision?" or "What are the consequences of not spending enough time growing the company?" Even when Julie was looking at an area to improve, Bob showed her how to use one of her strengths—skills that she already possessed—to create better outcomes for herself in an entirely different arena. It was because of this that Julie was able to move through her feedback, zero in on four goals, and start listing actions.

The feedback indicated that Julie is seen by most of the board and members of the leadership team as being highly competent and respected in her field, a natural leader, participative, an excellent communicator and motivator, results-oriented, strategic, and honest. Messages for development fell into these categories:

- Delegate more to members of the leadership team, with special attention to clarifying expectations.

- Improve process and approach toward decision making (for major decisions) to make more timely decisions.

- Spend less time on staff issues and more time growing the company.

- Confront and better manage difficult people and situations.

Being high in emotional intelligence, Julie embraced the feedback with little surprise. Yet, as she reviewed the findings before her next meeting with Bob, she felt stuck. She is a believer in participative management. So how can she make decisions faster without becoming less participative? She knows she has to confront the difficult board member (and several other difficult situations on the job), but how can she overcome her fears? And how can she take the time to delegate and establish clear expectations when she is already drowning in staff work? She needed to construct a plan.

Making It Real

This chapter discussed data-gathering methods, and the technical and conversational qualities necessary for higher levels of understanding. It also showed why having a feedback mindset and courage to give, receive, and redirect feedback is an important ingredient for a successful feedback process. Lastly, to create an environment that supports individuals and teams, the environment has to be invited into the process. We saw how including and thanking others, and demonstrating appreciation for their feedback, begins a cycle of support that allows change to happen. Please reflect on this chapter and develop ideas for how to incorporate what you've learned into your daily work.

1. Imagine a situation in which you have given or received feedback that was not done well.

2. Describe the scenario in terms of what was said and done: data-gathering method, attitude, language used, and results.
   - Scenario:

   - Language:

3. Based on what you read in this chapter, develop a goal for how you would like that scenario and similar scenarios to be handled in the future; then indicate new language that could be used in this scenario that would support your goal.
   - Goal:

   - New language:

5

Create Options and Construct a Plan

At this point in the process, the coachee has received feedback and you have supported the coachee's journey to a higher level of understanding through reflection and making connections among the data points. It is now time to formulate more specific goals and create an action plan. This chapter will follow a structured action plan, as shown in Table 5-1.

This is merely one way to design a plan. You may want to collapse the chart into only three columns (Goal, Actions to Take, and Status) or use a more fluid plan, such as the mindmap approach shown in Figure 5-1.

The impetus behind an action plan is to use a written method to capture thoughts. It is through the process of writing down actions, feelings, results, and ideas that the brain focuses, embraces the process, and assists the coachee in making things happen. The written format encourages reflection, and through reflection, learning happens. Practice and reflection hardwires learning in the brain. Without a mechanism to hardwire the brain, messages and learning pass through without moving us to action.

Table 5-1. Example Coaching Action Plan

Goals and Areas for Development	Desired Outcomes and Measures	Actions	Coaching Notes
Time management: Improve time management to incorporate administrative, interactive job components.	Within three months: » Administrative projects are completed on time. » Staff is taking on activities without my assistance. » New mechanism and meeting structure in place for staff updates and coaching	» By next session, choose a definitive time every week to sit down and plan my week. Use a weekly planner to see entire week and month at a glance. Have this in place and be ready to discuss at least one personal planning time with coach by next session. » Schedule time to do paperwork. Tell others that I shouldn't be interrupted except for stipulated emergency reasons. Use a clock to keep time structured. » Be ready to show coach the planned sessions on the calendar and have completed one such paperwork session before next coaching session.	» Be aware of my tendency to run out of my office and solve problems. Don't open door during planning time until alarm rings. » Keep in mind that my job is to not only be on the front line, but also organize the administrative structure. » Remember that I can have more time to manage and coach when I empower others to do more of the work themselves.

Adapted from Bianco-Mathis, Roman, and Nabors (2008)

Figure 5-1. Mindmap Action Plan Approach

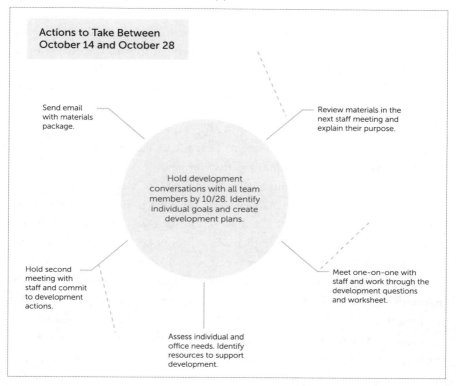

Actions to Take Between October 14 and October 28

Send email with materials package.

Review materials in the next staff meeting and explain their purpose.

Hold development conversations with all team members by 10/28. Identify individual goals and create development plans.

Hold second meeting with staff and commit to development actions.

Meet one-on-one with staff and work through the development questions and worksheet.

Assess individual and office needs. Identify resources to support development.

For example, you can read a book on time management and say to yourself, "Yep, that's what I really need to do to better manage my time." The knowledge is in your head. Then what? Do you do it? You will not do it unless you create a plan that motivates you to put the knowledge into practice. Here's another example. We all have the knowledge of what is necessary to maintain a healthy weight. Does that mean we do it? What does it take to stay on a diet? A clear, positively stated goal and articulated steps to achieve it. That's what an action plan and coaching toward that action plan provides.

A coachee may be writing a summary of a certain interaction and find himself having an aha moment: "Wow. Look at that. I didn't realize I was angry when Donna approached me—and she had nothing to do with my anger. And yet, I took out my anger on her. I need to be more aware of that. Let me list some things I might do next time so I can share this with my coach."

And as you will see, using an action plan assists in punctuating movement and benchmarking achievements along the path to the goal. We often underestimate and undervalue our movement toward a result because the end result is not in sight. Noting gradual movement toward the goal reminds the coachee that success is happening, one step at a time. This needs to be acknowledged and celebrated—and it can only happen with written documentation. This is an important concept to share with coachees who may initially balk at following an action plan, keeping notes, or maintaining a journal. What's in their heads needs to be made explicit—or it stays stuck in their heads with no active, mindful reflection.

Whether you use the template in Table 5-1 or some other shortened version, all the data points within each column need to be addressed through dialogue and further note taking. The action plan becomes an anchor that allows the coach and coachee to focus on reflection and movement from one meeting to the next. It forces conversations to be more meaningful when specifics can be noted and analyzed, as opposed to coachees coming to meetings with vague comments, such as, "Yes, I did that. It was great," "This isn't working. I don't see any progress," or, "Yep, thanks. I'll do that next time."

When you read through the example plan, you can see further notes, explanations, and analysis included. This is a living document. If either you or the coachee has ideas between coaching meetings—or want to make sure a point made during dialogue is noted—adding such information to the action plan should be done.

Lastly, who should fill out the action plan? We have talked to many coaches, and their answers vary. The most prevalent and useful seems to be a joint effort between the coach and coachee. Usually, the coachee is given a blank template and is asked to do a first draft. Then through further questioning and interaction with the coach, the action plan takes shape and becomes a working document.

Goals and Measures

By establishing goals, the coachee can develop specific objectives and actions to populate her action plan. The concept of goals was first used as part of the management by objectives movement in the early 1980s with Peter Drucker.

This included the idea of establishing SMART goals—goals that are specific, measurable, agreed upon, realistic, and time-bound. You can find various versions of the SMART concept in management literature; some authors use different wording for each letter, but the intent and use of the concept remains the same.

Because the concept of setting goals has been around for so long, we often forget how important it is to set goals. Let's put this in context: Humans are the only species that can establish conscious goals (Parker 2015). Think about that a second. Stephen Covey (quoted in Falconer 2017) put it very poetically: "Goals are what take us forward in life; they are the oxygen to our dreams." It is goals that target our journey, help us overcome procrastination, and motivate us when things get tough. That is why Weight Watchers encourages you to put a picture of a "healthy version" of yourself on the refrigerator, construction companies design models and place them in the front of the buying center, and corporations develop visions and strategic goals.

In coaching, we encourage you not to get overly concerned whether you designate a useful action statement as being a goal or a task or action step. More important is to write it all down. That is why we have chosen to use the terms *area to work*, *goals and objectives*, and *actions, steps, and behaviors*. If they are measurable and achievable—and designated actions between coaching meetings are noted and discussed—there is a path to success.

Table 5-2 shows different goal possibilities and characteristics. We will use this table to discuss the "musts" of goals, objectives, and actions. These points, originally described by Teri Belf and Giuseppe Meli (2011), provide a checklist that you and your coachee should follow.

Table 5-2. Sample Goals and Objectives

Coaching Goal	Measurable Objective
Improve presentation skills.	Adopt a presentation approach for the next board meeting that participants will rate as organized and focused on only four main points, and that results in follow-up actions on the part of the board.
Be more of a team player.	For the next three months, have selected colleagues keep a record of when I ask more questions, acknowledge the ideas of others before making a final decision, listen with intent, and use the dialogue skills of balanced approach, switch shoes, and problem solving.

Table 5-2. Sample Goals and Objectives (cont.)

Coaching Goal	Measurable Objective
Complete all action items from the organizational survey that affect my team.	Meet with team over three sessions (to be completed by June 15) and develop actions plan with measurable outputs for the first four items over which we have full accountability. For the fifth item, work with accounting and develop a win-win format for completing reports on time. For the last item, formulate win-win ideas for my team and sales to work more in collaboration, and work with the directors to formulate a plan for supporting this effort.

Adapted from Bianco-Mathis, Roman, and Nabors (2008)

First, goals and objectives must include desired results and a future state. The goal is not just to improve presentation skills. Rather, the parameter of "so that listeners rate the presentation as organized, focused on only three or four points, and actionable" brings a measurable structure to the goal that fits that particular need and culture. In this case, by explicitly stating the desired future state, the coachee is also stipulating the measure. This parameter emphasizes the future focus of coaching. It is movement forward toward future performance, not a judgment of the past. This will become very important when we look at more innovative performance management systems in chapter 7.

Second, they must be phrased using positive language. As we will see in chapter 7, using positive phrasing is something the brain "likes." The brain picks up on the positive, gets energized, and wants to be part of the action. Moving toward the positive is much more energizing than running away from the negative. Thus, "Develop presentations that clearly stipulate three key points" is a lot more powerful than saying, "Make sure my presentations are not disorganized."

Third, ensure that the action and results are within the coachee's control—and stipulate parameters that clarify the constraints. The third example in Table 5-2 illustrates this well. A goal that is hard to reach and constricted by unacknowledged challenges sets the coachee up for failure before he even starts.

Fourth, goals need to be measurable. All the examples in Table 5-2 are measurable. A fallacy that persists is that measurable means there must be numbers or statistics. This is not true. Basically, something is measurable if it can be observed—seen, felt, smelled. This requires that the form or method of measurement needs to be indicated: an on-the-spot survey, follow-up phone calls, a specially designed feedback sheet, being observed, checkmarks on a calendar. If nothing exists, it needs to be created. The excuse "we have no way to measure that" is just that—an excuse.

Actions and Field Practice

The development of action steps can be a fun process. This step is sometimes referred to as homework or field practice because it takes place between the coaching meetings—actions the coachee takes to try out new behaviors, practice the use of skills that initially may feel foreign, or apply further new ideas. Questions that could be helpful during this phase include:

- What can you do at your next meeting that would demonstrate this behavior?
- When can you give this a try?
- If you did that, how would it help you meet your goal?
- What three actions might you take that others would notice?
- How might your staff react to that? What obstacles might arise? Would it be helpful to role-play?
- What resources might you reach out for that would support you in this effort?
- How might you gather more data about that?
- Is there something you can use that would remind you to ask more questions?

Action steps and field practice are benchmarking activities—proverbial baby steps toward the desired goal. For example, instead of suggesting that a coachee ask a question before barking out orders, you might assign homework during which she merely notes how many times she "barks out orders" during the next week, while tracking what was in her mind, what she was feeling, and the results of her "barking." That's all. Just the mindful "stop and look at what you are doing" is a major accomplishment in connecting a field assignment to a goal.

A partial list of field assignments includes the following:

- **Journaling:** Try the new behavior three times and after each situation, note what you did or said, what the reactions were, and what you learned.

- **Assignments:** Have a conversation with a co-worker; conduct interviews with three partners who got promoted last year; role-play the process with two of your co-workers.
- **Feedback:** Ask a co-worker to observe you at the next meeting and then give you feedback.
- **Props:** Take a notebook and consider it your "don't interrupt" prop. Whenever you want to interrupt someone, write it down instead and then later bring it up.
- **Research:** Find three articles, videos, and experts on the skill set you wish to develop, such as strategic planning, and take notes on how you can incorporate those ideas into your process.
- **Skill practice:** Instead of conducting an entire follow-up survey, start by asking one question at the end of every conversation or phone call: "Was my advice helpful to you?"
- **Role models:** Find three people who are really good at networking. Watch them. Take notes and bring your ideas to your next meeting.

Case Study

While Julie can't wait to do the work of coaching, she is not sure how to make progress. She knows that maintaining the status quo is not the answer. Her overall goals for coaching are at the front of her mind:

- Become a better leader who develops other strong leaders.
- Grow the company.
- Make timely decisions while still building participative teams.
- Manage difficult situations with such confidence and grace that they result in higher levels of understanding and agreement.

During the last coaching meeting, with Bob's help, Julie analyzed the pros and cons of moving forward on different aspects of the feedback and decided on four key goals from which to develop an action plan. At first, she struggled writing the goals, but Bob encouraged her to picture herself six months from now as perfectly exhibiting the behaviors that demonstrate the desired outcome. What is she doing and saying? How are people reacting? How does she feel? What results is she achieving?

This "future picture" exercise enabled her to more easily define measurable goals and objectives and prioritize them.

Now what? For homework, she was supposed to jot down some concrete actions to achieve her top goal. Julie reread her notes from the last meeting, and it hit her: Bob recommended that she interview two or three members of her leadership team—and perhaps one of her outside contacts—who are admired for their decision-making abilities. She should ask them for advice:

- How do you make decisions?

- What do you do to ensure that your decisions are timely?

- How do you involve others to encourage buy-in? Do you use one method or several?

- Having observed me for the past year, what can I do more of or less of that would help with my decision making?

- How do you deal with the possibility of making a decision that's wrong? Have you ever made one? How did you handle it?

Julie likes her list of questions and knows exactly whom she is going to talk to. She feels confident about approaching Tom, Sara, and Tamara. Tom had tried to give Julie some feedback about her decision making last time they had coffee together, but she had been too busy to listen. Julie also knows she should reach out to the best decision maker on her team, Nick, but she feels uncomfortable doing so. Nick tends to be very judgmental—something Julie has been meaning to address with him (another one of those "confront and better manage difficult situations" that she hasn't moved on). Julie reminds herself of the importance of embracing vulnerability to engage and grow. As Bob has helped her realize, it is her job to role-model the appropriate way to solicit and receive feedback. She wants to make that a norm for the entire organization. So, she adds Nick to the list. Julie hopes that with the notes she intends to collect, she can determine concrete actions to discuss and expand on with Bob. Then, as agreed in her coaching contract, she jots down her thoughts and insights as she moves through the coaching steps. As Bob keeps emphasizing, "We learn through reflection."

Making It Real

As this chapter illustrated, the development of an action plan is the cornerstone of formal coaching. However, it can be easily seen how managers and colleagues can take the concept of action planning and apply it in informal coaching settings. A plan can simply be a scheduled time to complete a task toward a desired goal, such as "Meet with Sally to get tips on completing assessment reports," or putting checks on a calendar every time the coachee appropriately asks questions at a meeting. Adopting the habit of thinking in terms of SMART goals and objectives naturally leads to results that you and the coachee can see, feel, and track, as opposed to wishful thinking and anecdotal outcomes.

Also noted in this chapter was the necessity of being creative in your action steps and practice. Actions should support growth and at the same time be tailored to what the coachee will most likely do. This may include reading a book, watching an online webinar, or having a series of conversations with six different people. Slowly, through field work, the coachee can gain strength and confidence in moving forward and experiencing success at a new skill level. Please reflect on this chapter and develop ideas for how to incorporate what you've learned into your daily work.

1. Think of a scenario in which a goal was not achieved because of lack of focus and mindfulness. In this situation, you may use yourself or someone you have formally or informally coached.

2. Describe the scenario in terms of initial thoughts or notions around wanting something to be achieved, the lack of progress or results, and the reasoning behind the inaction. Then list any keywords, phrases, or mental thoughts that supported the failure to reach the goal.

    - Scenario:

    - Language:

3. Based on what you read in this chapter, develop a goal for the scenario that possesses all the components of a SMART goal, with supporting language and actions that would more likely lead to tangible results.

    - SMART goal and actions:

6

Commit to Action and Celebrate Success

You and the coachee are now centered with a working plan. On the formal end of the coaching continuum, you and the coachee have agreed to meet regularly for a period of three to six months or more to move toward the desired goals. Toward the middle of the coaching continuum, a manager and employee might develop a growth action plan to guide four to six development meetings over the year. And on the informal end of the coaching continuum, a manager might make some notes on his calendar to follow up on the "in the moment" coaching session he had with a colleague. In all these cases, there is some documentation to guide further discussions.

Now what? In an ideal situation, the coachee embraces the ongoing work required in coaching, does all the fieldwork in between each meeting, demonstrates success in accomplishing small steps forward, and can problem solve and work through all challenges successfully. In real life, coachees often must navigate both external and internal challenges. External challenges may include an unexpected increase in work load, unanticipated deadlines, difficult employees, or a major reorganization. Internal challenges may include lack of self-awareness, self-doubt, fear of failure, or impatience. All these internal challenges are types of resistance.

Resistance

The classic definition of resistance is to push back or work against. A less well-known definition includes the word *protect*. You may wonder, why would a coachee resist the opportunity to move forward in pursuit of goals that he has said are important? Why might a coachee suddenly demonstrate a reticence to do the work she said was her number-one priority? Perhaps they are protecting the vision of themselves that they have become comfortable with. Remember, you are supporting them in making changes, and that means letting go of behaviors that they may feel have contributed to their success to this point. They are comfortable with these behaviors. It is possible that they may have second thoughts. Change requires a lot of work. And letting go of what we know can be scary.

So, how can you help your client or co-worker in a coaching situation? The answers to these questions can be found in three of the most common forms of resistance you may encounter when coaching: ego, fear, and impatience (Staub 1996).

Let's look first at ego. Ego is present in all human beings. On a good day, it can give us confidence and support our efforts to try new things. It can also get in the way of us taking responsibility for our contribution in a given situation and lead to us blaming others. This inhibits our learning. Successful coaches are able to create a safe space for their coachees so that they can consider how they may have contributed to a given situation and what they might do differently to achieve the result they would prefer. Asking questions and considering pros and cons of a given action can help.

Fear keeps us paralyzed. It prevents us from hearing feedback and from sharing feedback. When a coachee is afraid, she cannot hear important messages and more important, she will not act on them. Asking questions about best and worst case outcomes and how to ensure the former can help. Reality testing is also a powerful tool to overcome fear.

Impatience recasts ego and fear and creates an impossible scenario in which the coachee wants to effect a change immediately. Rather than allowing time to practice and perfect a skill or demonstrating consistency in applying a given behavior, she wants to demonstrate new behavior and receive acknowledgment of the behavior overnight. This is not likely to happen. As a coach, you will have to create a system with your coachee to encourage continued practice and reinforce the new behavior as it is being practiced. Recognize that coachees are working to add new behaviors or, as David Rock (2006) notes, they are "creating new wiring." This takes time.

Table 6-1 outlines some of the more common resistance statements you may encounter and several optional dialogue questions you might use to counter the resistance. Study these and add your own as you master the art and science of coaching in your work.

Table 6-1. Helping Coachees Get Unstuck

Coachee Resistance	Possible Coach Responses
There are no good options.	» What are the consequences of doing nothing? » Let's lay out all options. We can pick the one that pays off the most.
I tried that. It doesn't work.	» What would work? » How is this situation the same or different as before?
Setting goals is a waste of time. Things change too fast here.	» Are goals helpful to you in general? » How can goals be created that can withstand change?
It's not my fault.	» How does blaming others help you?
There's no time.	» What can you do in the time you do have? » From experience, how long does it usually take for a new habit to take hold?
I don't want to hurt her feelings.	» How likely is that to happen? How do you know? » What are the consequences of not giving her this information?
I don't want to rock the boat.	» What would happen if you rocked the boat? » How is this rocking the boat? » What are the consequences of doing nothing?
You don't understand how things work around here.	» That may be true. What does it take to be effective here? » How might you take this and modify it to fit how things are done around here?

Adapted from Bianco-Mathis, Roman, and Nabors (2008)

Bringing in the Environment

Chapter 4 emphasized the importance of "bringing in the environment" to create a fertile ground for coaching to stick. No matter whether the coaching is formal or informal, the coach should encourage the coachee to bring the environment into the process. In an informal setting, this can be as simple as suggesting that the coachee talk to someone who has skill sets, information, or connections that can assist the coachee in achieving goals. Often, the coachee merely needs a reminder that reaching out and asking others to share their strengths is a readily available resource. Other times, the coachee may need to be encouraged by role-playing the words or envisioning the process for approaching others.

It is very useful—especially with more formal coaching situations—to develop a more structured tool for engaging the environment. Inviting others into the process can be measurable, as demonstrated in Table 6-2.

Table 6-2. Direct Observation Feedback

Behavior	1/10	1/17	1/24	1/31	2/7
Is open to new ideas					
Clarifies who will do what and when					
Encourages open discussion					
Ensures participants equal airtime					
Clarifies actions to be taken					
Reviews quality criteria					
Reviews customer care feedback					

Adapted from Bianco-Mathis, Roman, and Nabors (2008)

Such a tool should be tailored to the specific behaviors pertinent to the coachee. You would work with the coachee to develop no more than six key observable behaviors that the coachee can then ask others to watch out for. Notice that the intent is that the observer is being asked to recognize the new behavior. Remember the "Getting Support From Others" section in chapter 4? By asking members of the coachee's environment to concentrate on the new behavior, it opens and forces their brains to change existing labels. It is an elegant way to seed the environment toward accepting and noting new characteristics. By asking members of the environment to actively participate in the process, they now have a role to play and will be more inclined to help the coachee succeed. Obviously, this method also keeps the coachee on track because she knows others are looking for those behaviors that lead to her desired future state.

The coachee should be encouraged to choose observers who can be balanced and truthful. They should also be involved enough in the coachee's sphere of work to realistically assess different situations. The wording a coachee can use to invite observers into the process might go something like this:

Terry, because you're a colleague who sits with me on several commit-
tees, I'd like to ask you to help me with something and I'm hoping you
can support me. As you may know, I'm working with an executive
coach on my leadership development. I have identified—through some
great feedback—four skill sets that I am going to be more mindfully
demonstrating. I've developed this chart that outlines the observable
behaviors. What I'm asking is that you keep this checklist with you
and observe me during our times together. When you notice me exhibiting these actions, please note the date, situation, what I said and did,
and the results. Next month I'll come by and ask what you have to
share. Would you be open to helping me out with this?

The observation document can include not only positive events, but also
another column for "Could have done better." If included, the purpose is to
remind the coachee (and the observer) that improvement is a work in progress.
The coach and coachee can decide on which approach to use.

Celebrating Success

By knowing the coachee's agenda, you are in the position to support,
acknowledge, cheer, and congratulate the coachee on facing fears, taking steps
forward, repeatedly trying out new behaviors, and reflecting on his actions.
Studies have shown that one of the top three motivators in the workplace
is acknowledgment—not money, promotion, or even benefits (they are still
important, but they are not motivators) (Lipman 2014). And as a formal or
informal coach, support and encouragement can and should be given freely.

The action plan illustrates a succession of baby steps toward the desired
goal, and it must be punctuated like a birthday, an anniversary, or a gradu-
ation. Even if a coaching relationship is going to continue beyond the initial
negotiated timeframe, it is useful to pick a time (three months to a year) for
which a definitive checkpoint is scheduled—a time to stop and bask in the
positive forward movement.

During the status check, guide the coachee toward one of these options:

- **Continuation of coaching at a higher level.** This might involve
  establishing new goals or adding additional objectives to the
  process with new targets and timelines.

- **Assessing how the coaching is going** and whether it might be useful for the coachee to work with another coach to be supported through another set of eyes.
- **Assessing whether it is time to stop formal coaching** and have the coachee move forward on his own, applying coaching skill sets to his own growth.

The status check might go smoothly or may be a time during which the coachee exhibits resistance. Supporting the coachee through "going it alone" might involve role-playing and action planning. This is also a good time to remind the coachee that she already has all the skills and tools necessary to not only coach herself, but also others. By engaging in a coaching process, she has had to absorb, practice, and hardwire coaching skills into her own brain. To help the coachee realize that she is set to take on this new challenge, you might ask:

- What have you learned by engaging in a coaching process?
- If you were to coach a colleague, staff member, or boss, how would you go about that?
- If you were going to describe the coaching process to someone, how would you characterize the benefits and challenges?
- What benefit do you see in everyone using coaching behaviors within your organization?
- What kind of support groups might you form or engage in to hone and continue to strengthen your coaching skills?
- What formal situations might you create to continue progress along your own action plan?
- How might you partner with someone else in the organization to support mutual coaching?
- In what ways can you role-model good coaching techniques— in what situations?
- Let's say it is one year from now and a co-worker says that you are a good example of someone who knows how to coach herself and others. What would you be doing and saying to foster that kind of feedback?
- If you were on a team that was going to institute structures and policies to build an entire coaching organization, what ideas might you have? In what ways might you begin to influence the organization toward that goal?

Case Study

Let's revisit our executive, Julie, as she grapples with one of her goals.

Bob: Last time we spoke, you were going to speak up at the board meeting. The intent was that you would set the stage for problem solving when your difficult board member, Matt, went on the attack.

Julie: Yes, that was the intent. I didn't do it.

Bob: What happened?

Julie: Matt started in with his criticism of the numbers, and I froze. The role play you and I had last month kept playing in my head, but none of the words came out. Luckily, David was there to keep things moderately calm, and I emerged with only a few bumps and bruises.

Bob: I'm glad to hear that the role play we had was playing in your head. That's a step in the direction of your goal. Think about that. At the last board meeting your mind was totally blank, and you were too angry and upset to speak up. This is progress. What needs to happen for those words to leave your head and come out of your mouth?

Julie: Good question. As the words were swirling around my head, I was feeling scared and ashamed.

Bob: Those are strong emotions. Tell me more.

Julie: I was scared that Matt would pounce as soon as I began to speak. And then, because I wasn't speaking, I felt ashamed for not being the kind of leader that could handle a bully like Matt.

Bob: If I put myself in your shoes, I can understand both of those feelings. First, you know what it's like to be attacked by Matt, and it's not pleasant. Fearing that scenario is perfectly normal. Second, having this picture in your head of the leader you want to be—and realizing that you are not yet living up to that picture—can be discouraging. Share with me how my explanation is aligned or not with what you were feeling.

Julie: I think you captured it well. And because of those feelings, I became overwhelmed and, quite frankly, froze. This is hard. After our role play, I thought I was ready to go in there and be strong. I'm now wondering if I will ever get there.

Bob: You'll get there. The process may be slower than you'd like, but that's why you're engaged in coaching! How long did it take you to get this position? Did you just decide to become a CEO and the next day you got the job? How about riding a bike? Did you just hop on the bike with no training wheels and ride perfectly from day one? I know you're a good tennis player. What stages did you go through to get better at tennis?

Julie: OK, let's see. . . . (Julie goes through her history of lessons, practice, and working with challenging partners.) I get your point.

Bob: Exactly. Your ability to stand your own ground with the likes of Matt will require diligence, practice, and time. What are some things you might do to remind yourself that this is a marathon and not a sprint to the finish line?

Julie: Huh. I like that analogy. Actually, that is one thing I can do—picture myself running through the twists and turns of a marathon. That can help. I think I want to talk to you about breaking this down into even smaller steps. Facing that fear is really holding me back.

Bob: OK. Let's revisit the future picture you have in your head. You are sitting in the next board meeting and Matt goes on the attack. You are strong. You know your work, results, and skills are exemplary and that you are moving the company forward. You have developed a worksheet that outlines his typical hot buttons and . . .

As this scenario demonstrates, Julie is experiencing the resistance characteristics of fear and impatience. She expresses her fear of Matt interrupting her. She expresses her impatience with her inability to respond to Matt using the role play she worked on with Bob. Note how Bob uses the following techniques to help Julie overcome her resistance:

- He acknowledges and legitimizes the feelings as perfectly normal and human.
- He recognizes the evolution in her thought process.

- He makes the resistance discussable.
- He uses an analogy to reframe the approach.
- He suggests that Julie develop tools and resources to use on her journey.
- He helps Julie envision what success looks like: revisits and further solidifies the future picture.
- He brings perspective to the entire incident.
- He encourages Julie to remember and bring to bear other times in her life when persistence and time were needed to reach a goal (mental connections).

Note the wording Bob used previously when Julie was feeling stuck:

> **Bob:** I'm glad to hear that the role play we had was playing in your head. That's a step in the direction of your goal. Think about that. At the last board meeting your mind was totally blank and you were too upset to speak up.

Even though this was a baby step in terms of the overall goal, Bob was mindful to shine a light on the fact that it was a step forward. Bob is doing his job as Julie's coach in keeping a safe space within which she can share her thinking, feeling, and incremental progress. He acknowledges her for taking steps to move closer to her goal. He acknowledges her courage in so doing. And, he helps her work through her plan for next steps. Julie has the opportunity to reveal what happened when she planned to take certain actions and did not. She has the chance to talk through how she felt and how those feelings got in her way. She has the chance to reframe her feelings. She then continues in her thinking and can consider other times when she pursued a goal and it took several tries. As Julie and Bob leave the coaching meeting, Julie feels fully prepared with a plan to move forward.

Making It Real

As we all know from our own growth endeavors, resistance is often around the corner ready to thwart the progress we are making. This chapter looked closely at how ego, fear, and impatience can create personal challenges while we are also trying to work through the constraints of uncooperative colleagues, difficult direct reports, and tense organizational situations. It discussed how to help coachees work through getting unstuck and support them as they move toward their desired goals and practice techniques to stay on track.

At this stage in the coaching process, it is important for the coachee to ask several members of his environment to observe and note times when the coachee exhibits new behaviors. Such an exercise hardwires the behavior not only for the coachee, but also for those who may tend to hold on to previously held perceptions. In the end, the coachee invites the environment to travel on the same development journey.

This chapter also covered the necessity of celebrating success and acknowledging even small steps as progress. It is the job of the coach to punctuate each practice, experience, and learning from one meeting to the next. Lastly, the chapter discussed how the coach should end the coaching engagement, helping the coachee build a plan for continuing the coaching process on her own—develop action plans, track progress, conduct field practice, create supportive tools, and embody coaching as a normal way of going about continuous improvement. This discipline tends to create future coaches and an entire coaching organization. Please reflect on this chapter and develop ideas for how to incorporate this learning into your daily work.

Think of a situation during which someone you were trying to help exhibited resistance and you were not able to move them beyond the resistance:

1. Describe the scenario in terms of the type of resistance, what they said and did, what you said and did, and the outcomes.
   - Scenario (circumstances, type of resistance, behaviors, outcomes):

   - Language (what and how things were said):

2. Based on what you read in this chapter, develop a goal for how you would like that scenario (and similar scenarios) to be handled in the future; then, indicate new language that could be used in the scenario that would support your goal.
   - Goal: When supporting people exhibiting resistance . . .

   - New language:

PART 3:
Building a Coaching Culture

In part 3, you will learn how an organization can mindfully create a coaching culture that permeates the entire enterprise. In addition, you will be equipped with the necessary tools and strategies to sustain a coaching mindset over time. Finally, you will discover what a coaching organization can look like. What would a person need to see and hear to walk into an organization and say, "Wow, it is obvious that the traditions, language, results, stories, and 'how things get done' are all based on the principles and practices of coaching"? The major strategy to achieve this goal is to design and implement a systems approach.

The first step is to define a coaching culture, "where all the infrastructures facilitate and reward everyone to learn, practice, and engage in mindful coaching conversations to get work done, accomplish goals, and reach both personal and strategic growth and success" (Bianco-Mathis and Nabors 2016, 2). Chapter 7, "Implementing a Systems Infrastructure," outlines a process for building a coaching culture—one that includes a perfect storm of the popular learning and organization development research of recent years; namely, but not limited to, emotional intelligence, employee engagement, strategic planning, monthly coaching meetings instead of yearly appraisals, apps for in-the-moment feedback, and change management. Finally, chapter 8, "Looking to the Future," imagines workplaces to come and outlines how they will likely evolve as more individuals practice dialogue and coaching, making organizations and the individuals within them curious, collaborative, and strong.

7

Implementing a Systems Infrastructure

An early definition of organization development (OD) is "an effort planned, organizationwide, and managed from the top to increase organization effectiveness and health through planned interventions in the organization's processes using behavioral-science knowledge" (Beckhard 1969, 9). More recent definitions—based on many years of practice and research—sound more like, "Organization development is the process of increasing organizational effectiveness and facilitating personal and organizational change through interventions driven by social and behavioral science knowledge" (Anderson 2015, 3).

The main difference between the old and new definition is that OD can happen anywhere in an organization. It can happen on the division, department, or group level and does not have to come from the top of the organization. Any person within an organization can apply OD skills and methods, just as anyone within an organization can begin to use coaching methods.

After 30 years in the field, we have found that the number one issue with many OD efforts is the lack of a systems approach. Instead of building an infrastructure of actions, they institute quick fixes.

If you and your organization want to conduct an organizational analysis to figure out why the new performance appraisal or technology system isn't working, the restructuring or merger is not producing adequate results, or the new hiring system isn't increasing engagement, you will likely find instead an inadequate support system to sustain the very goal of the change itself. Imagine a stool with only one leg, a car with little gas in the tank, or a broken arm trying to heal with a makeshift sling. You may succeed for a short period of time, but eventually your luck will run dry and you will find yourself no better off than before the change initiative. At that point, leaders turn around and say, "What happened? Why isn't this working?"

Using a Systems Model

By using a systems approach, practitioners can increase the chances of influencing organizational change. Let's take the following organizational goal: "Increase the health of employees to better manage health costs, reduce absenteeism, and mitigate stress in the workplace." To achieve this, the company will:

- Conduct a yearly health fair.
- Offer a series of online courses on stress management.
- Include health impact questions in the yearly climate survey and a separate survey specifically tailored to the relationship of participating in company health programs and bottom-line impact.

The first health fair is a great success and in the initial six months, 100 of 3,000 people take advantage of the stress courses. As the year goes on, only a trickle of people participate in the courses, and attendance at the second health fair is half that of the first. The surveys indicate minimal impact. What happened? The program merely limped along because a systems approach was not used in the design and implementation stages. Here is what a systems effort might look like:

- a yearly health fair with tests that earn you points and lead to lower health insurance payments
- a monthly, company-wide video program on health and stress reduction ideas, with the company CEO taking part in the panel
- the introduction of a balanced work-life policy with guidelines for every department to follow
- a monthly online newsletter on health issues pertaining to company population and culture, with statistics on health plans and competitors
- stress workout seminars once a year, during which intact teams discuss and brainstorm ways to reduce stress within their own team and work area.

This is a systems approach. In the previous example, every pertinent "system" component within the organization is included in the implementation, such as:

- budget and costs
- vision and values
- measurement and results
- benefits and compensation
- hiring and training
- technology.

Yet, even a well-planned design will not ensure successful results. The last ingredient necessary in a systems approach is that the plan includes as many behavioral hooks as possible. It is not enough to create vision and value statements that claim the importance of work-life balance. Nor is it enough to say, "Managers will follow the work-life balance guidelines." A plan doesn't become real unless there are accompanying benefits that affect employees, managers, and leaders concretely, such as managing your choices and gaining enough points to reduce your insurance payment, being measured as a good manager because you support work-life balance while also increasing the bottom line, and observing realistic role models. Even excellent ideas fail because people only went as far as throwing them out there, without planning them all the way to the behavioral hook.

So now go back and replace "stress and health management program" with "coaching culture program." The same rules and systems approach apply. Table 7-1 takes these key organization development components and applies them to the planning and implementation of a coaching culture. If you and a task force use this job aid as a road map, your plan will have a great chance for success: Create a vision, assess organizational readiness, design the components and implementation plan, and measure and sell the benefits. Consider how the Phillips Corporation—a machine-tool manufacturer and distributor in Maryland—leveraged these organization development components to become a coaching organization.

Table 7-1. How to Build a Coaching Organization

Developing a coaching organization involves a systems approach that begins with creating a vision and testing readiness and then moves toward implementation and measurement. This ensures that the infrastructure will continue to support a coaching culture over time.

Create a Vision
» What are the benefits of becoming a coaching organization?
» What departments and functions within the organization would support a coaching culture?
» How would such a culture support organizational goals and values? What organizational drivers will be fulfilled?
» What are the outcomes of becoming a coaching organization (for individuals, teams, and the entire organization)?
Assess Organizational Readiness
» Does the organization believe in continual learning and change, or is the status quo valued above all else? How does it demonstrate continual learning and change?
» Is there a history or precedent within the organization for allocating money toward development programs? Is it valued? Is it considered during the budgeting process?
» Does the culture support openness, confrontations, honesty, and dialogue—or is it best to withhold information?
» Are there other learning structures in the organization that the coaching program can depend on, be linked with, or build on? If so, what are they?
Assess Organizational Readiness
» Is the human resource department valued and credible, or is it seen as merely a compliance department?
» Are managers encouraged or measured on how well they develop others, communicate, and use a coaching approach? How so?
» How have other programs been successfully implemented within the organization?
Design the Components and Implementation of the Plan
» Who can become champions of a coaching organization and establish a task force?
» To what extent will the effort balance homegrown and outside experts?
» How will we define and outline each building block of a coaching organization: coaching tools and mindsets, dialogue, and supporting infrastructures?
» Given your organization and constraints, how will you develop a project plan with a schedule, meetings, owners, steps, roll-out plan, benchmarks, contingencies, and tracking?
» What criteria will be considered to determine how costs will be budgeted and tracked?

Design the Components and Implementation of the Plan
» Who will own and be administratively responsible for being in charge of the solution and transformation?
» What are the key benefits and success factors? What measuring tools (software, accounting support, surveys, focus groups, strategic alignment factors, bottom-line factors) do you need to continually track and sell the coaching organization activities?

Build a Coaching Organization
» How will information about the program be communicated in a multiyear communication plan?
» What data-gathering methods are the most appropriate? What costs are involved? How will data be shared, and with whom? Will you consider outside benchmarking, surveys, 360-degree instruments, inventories, supportive coaching software, and technology?

Measure and Sell the Benefits
» Who are the key stakeholders? How can you link your agenda to their agenda? What negotiation strategies will you use?
» How will you relate the coaching infrastructure components to all other pertinent programs and demonstrate mutual support?
» How are you planning for costs, both in the short and long term? Will you conduct a cost-benefit analysis?
» What supporting materials, charts, graphs, role descriptions, and other marketing materials will guide your implementation plan?

Measure and Sell the Benefits
» How will you measure key success factors of the coaching organization and publicize the results?
» What is the political climate within your organization? How will you plan for contingencies, formal and informal power channels, decision-maker involvement, and how things usually get done throughout the organization?

Adapted from Bianco-Mathis, Roman, and Nabors (2008)

Case Study

The Phillips Corporation is an international machine-tool distributor. A continuous learner, advocate of listening to feedback, and avid reader, CEO Alan Phillips decided to work with an executive coach. Alan became passionate about not only his own self-improvement but also making continuous feedback, stretch goals, dialogue, and high performance key aspects of his company's culture. He adopted the motto of "make it necessary" in building a successful company for organizational, personal, and community success. His vision is for everyone to be excited about coming to work.

With the use of outside consultants and himself as a role model of continuous self-improvement, Alan embarked on a plan to turn the internal spirit of Phillips around. He traveled to every site with a consultant, and they conducted dozens of half-day seminars on what it means to be a virtuoso at one's job, creating personal visions aligned with the company's vision, providing real feedback on real issues, formulating both work and personal goals that focus on accountability, and becoming an active player in perpetuating this culture every day with fellow associates.

An example of Alan's role-modeling was allowing one of his senior leaders to openly discuss the fact that one of Alan's emails was perceived as inconsiderate, counterproductive, and distrusting. The ensuing dialogue was intense and yet has become part of Phillips's cultural history. It took two years for the senior team to believe that Alan was serious and that he would live up to his promise that they would not be penalized for not meeting their stretch goals; rather, they would be rewarded for what they continually try to do to reach them.

After two years, productivity increased and infrastructures were instituted to feed the coaching mindset. These included:

- workshops in coaching and dialogue
- a performance management system based on real feedback and goal setting
- individual resources so all associates could benchmark their own job in the marketplace and come back with ideas for personal improvement and needed resources
- multiple vehicles for feedback
- coaching embedded in the recruitment process, with all candidates having to submit an essay on how they could add value to the organizational culture
- special coaching and yearlong leadership education for key stakeholders
- a mentoring program
- regular, virtual conversations between colleagues to share insights on selected leadership articles, books, and blogs

- an ambassador program in which associates become champions and coaches for others

- a leading-edge human resource team with a senior champion reporting directly to the president

- quarterly leadership dialogues with action planning on both business and culture goals.

The difference is palpable at the Phillips Corporation. You can see it in the company's vision, mission, and brand statement: "To be the best resource in manufacturing technology—virtuosos engaging in dialogue to create the better idea."

Linking Coaching to Neuroscience

As Daniel Goleman proclaimed almost 20 years ago in his book *Working With Emotional Intelligence*, "We're being judged by a new yardstick: not just by how smart we are, or by our training and expertise, but also by how well we handle ourselves and each other" (1998, 3). More recently, Kim Scott described a foundational challenge for leaders in her book, *Radical Candor*, saying, "Your ability to build trusting, human connections with the people who report directly to you will determine the quality of everything that follows" (2017, 8). Yet we are still faced with the challenge of "selling" the value of coaching behaviors. Perhaps neuroscience will prove to be a new weapon in the arsenal of practitioners who want to leverage everyday conversations in service to coaching cultures.

In *Quiet Leadership*, David Rock (2006) introduced a new approach to leadership. He took a scientific, practical approach and, as he explains, "deconstructed the 'code' behind those high-performance conversations that transformed people's performance." Seven years later, in his 2013 TEDx Talk, "Learning About the Brain Changes Everything," Rock described why learning about the brain helps people better understand themselves and others:

- **The novelty effect:** Something new captures people's attention and opens connections. People are more willing to listen to something new.

- **Tangibles are easier to see:** Linking specific biological research with relatable stories and examples helps people visualize and connect to the process being described.

- **Understanding experience leads to more choices:** If people appreciate the physiological impact of emotions on themselves and others, they are likely to behave more mindfully.

Better understanding can support increased buy-in. Individuals and teams can learn to create new neural pathways leading to new behaviors. What does this look like? Neuroscience—specifically, insights into how the brain focuses, learns, and moves toward or away from new learning experiences—is at the center of how coaching works. Utilizing neuroscience principles will support individuals and organizations to more readily build bridges (new behaviors) over established pathways (old behaviors) that are no longer serving them well. This is an exciting addition to the field. Neuroscience presents practical evidence (brain scans, blood pressure, hormone levels) demonstrating what happens inside the brain when individuals diligently choose and practice behaviors that move them closer to their goals. A review of neuroscience research demonstrates how it supports the essence of coaching and coaching cultures.

Hardwiring Coaching Mindsets and Tools

The tools in this book—the Seven Cs Coaching Map, the C-O-A-CH model, the building blocks of dialogue—equip you to create, practice, and perpetuate a coaching culture in your organization. To set yourself up for success, your move toward creating a coaching culture should be carefully explained, orchestrated, and staged over a period of one or two years.

What creative learning methods might be useful at this point? Consider our two company examples, Seyfarth Shaw in the introduction and Phillips Corporation in this chapter. People need to be trained, guided, and supported with coaching materials and job aids. Recent studies show that this is an area of opportunity for the field because only 42 percent of managers have received 125-200 hours of coach-specific training (ICF 2016). Some methods that you can make a part of your system planning are in Table 7-2.

Table 7-2. Hardwiring Coaching Techniques

» Develop intact group training in which teams or departments learn these concepts and practice them with real job scenarios.
» Train a core group of visible leaders to take part in teaching the coaching classes.

» Create and implement a one-day kickoff training day for all project teams that incorporates coaching methods and results.

» At all times, have each person on your executive team coaching junior managers.

» Create workshops with trained internal or external professionals (virtual or in person) in which participants bring real work activities and practice coaching approaches.

» Benchmark other companies that have coaching cultures. Visit and take videos. Stream these videos on your company intranet.

» Choose key influencers in the organization and give them more intense training than others so they can be role models and speak at events and special meetings.

» Develop your own company or organizational textbook or job aids for coaching.

» Institute a formal program for all director-level and above employees to receive 360-degree performance appraisals, with at least three built-in coaching sessions to review results and develop action plans.

» Conduct a pilot, widely advertise the results, and use it as a model to implement throughout the organization.

» Train in-house advanced coaches who can be available to support others who have coaching dilemmas.

» Widely distribute coaching articles.

» Conduct yearly coaching booster seminars for all departments with special seminars for leadership (guest coaching gurus in leadership).

» Separate all training so that there is field practice and peer coaching in between classes.

» Incorporate coach training into all management and leadership development programs.

» Tailor the coaching approach to specifically meet the needs of different roles in the organization (salespeople, administrators, global travelers, service providers, research teams, coders, engineers, HR professionals, strategic planners, finance people, and IT).

These learning activities should be rolled out at the same time you are building supporting vehicles—incorporating coaching into existing structures and creating new structures to sustain the coaching culture. As human beings, we don't embrace change until we have to actually live it—basically, until there are rewards or consequences for incorporating such change. Table 7-3 provides a list of examples (with important additional resources embedded in the list) you can adopt or morph to fit your organization.

These coaching structures do not require that everyone in an organization be a certified coach. Rather, having key learning professionals within such organizations attend coaching workshops, join coaching forums, build coaching tools and guidelines, educate all members in the organization, and tie coaching behaviors to strategic success will make the transition smoother. That way they can pass along the coaching mindset to everyone else in the organization.

Table 7-3. Sample Coaching Structures

» Publish a monthly coaching blog.
» Form coaching teams in which members coach one another.
» Have employees join local or international coaching organizations.
» Have employees get formal coaching certification.
» Integrate coaching into the hiring and onboarding process: Every new hire gets a coach for six months.
» Make coaching a part of your promotion process: Everyone who is promoted or affected by a job restructuring (no matter how high in the organization) works with a coach for three months.
» Form coaching book or article clubs, either in person or virtually.
» Form coaching round robin groups or partnerships (in person or virtual) in which participants share coaching stories and coach one another.
» Publish and formalize coaching guidelines (the coaching you have in your company, how to get a formal coach, ways to coach colleagues and peers, how to be a coaching manager, how coaching fits with other learning systems within your company, how you measure coaching).
» Teach all coachees how to become coaches themselves.
» Teach managers how to hold monthly sharing stories meetings.
» Provide guest speakers and coaching webinars on coaching practices.
» Publish internal coaching highlights and successes.
» Develop a resource for finding and using dialogue tools for a specific on-the-job scenario.
» Use an app for giving and receiving just-in-time, daily feedback.
» Eliminate the existing performance appraisal process and replace with monthly coaching checkups (coaching appraisals) and yearly summaries of value to the organization.
» Incorporate coaching behaviors and standards into job descriptions, performance goals, and compensation and rewards program.
» Incorporate coaching mindset into strategic plan, corporate vision, and organizational values.
» Incorporate coaching into employee handbooks and management guidelines.
» Create a coaching initiative that goes beyond organizational boundaries and into the community, such as with schools, community groups, youth services, and religious organizations.
» Include fun and experiential activities so coaching and dialogue become engrained in the culture. Have contests, comic strips, and props that signify that you are a coaching organization.

Transforming Culture Through Coaching Appraisals

One of the more leading-edge coaching solution tools in Table 7-3 is the coaching appraisal. Dismantling your company's performance appraisal process and introducing an entirely new program demonstrates how one carefully orchestrated initiative can influence an entire culture faster than a "throw darts at the wall" method. Deloitte kick-started this notion of a new performance management approach (Buckingham and Goodall 2015) and other companies have followed suit (Shook 2015). So what does this really mean, and what does it actually look like?

It has led to the trend of throwing out existing performance appraisals and replacing them with monthly coaching checkups—as being used by Deloitte, Gap, Juniper, Cargill, Accenture, and Adobe (Rock, Davis, and Jones 2014; Impraise 2016). As David Rock and colleagues explain, organizations are adopting what neuroscience research has proven and are adopting "growth mindset performance techniques" rather than the existing "fixed mindset" approaches. Organizations are realizing that getting everyone up to speed on coaching skills is now not just "a nice way to give feedback and develop people" but instead a major component for more realistically assessing performance and ultimately organizational success.

Research indicates that 95 percent of managers are dissatisfied with their performance management systems, and 90 percent of HR leaders believe that performance appraisals do not yield accurate information (Rock, Davis, and Jones 2014). Existing appraisal systems embody the following less than desirable, noncoaching characteristics:

- idiosyncratic rater effect
- form focused, not people focused
- judgmental, not supportive or developmental
- time consuming
- rating focused, not future focused
- anxiety driven, not engaging
- less meaningful in today's fast-paced, service-oriented institutions
- forced to coincide with conceptual pay models as opposed to true performance.

Instead, what's being recommended are very simple periodic coaching sessions. For example, you can build the coaching appraisals around monthly sessions and have both the supervisor and employee gather data in a variety of ways. Questions for the supervisor to guide the discussion include (and note, this is a two-way discussion):

- What's working and should be continued?
- What can you do more of to be effective?
- What can you do less of to be more effective?
- What will you be doing over the next month to address this?
- What can I do to assist you with this?

Then, at the end of the performance cycle, the manager can submit a one-page assessment that addresses the employee's overall value to the organization:

1. Given what I know about this person's performance, and if it were my money, I would award this person the highest possible compensation [measures overall performance and unique value].
2. Given what I know of this person's performance, I would always want him or her on my team [measures ability to work with others].
3. This person is at risk for low performance [identifies problems that might harm the customer or team].
4. This person is ready for a growth opportunity today [measures potential].

Other companies are embracing new software and social media apps that allow them to give feedback to one another (up, down, and sideways) in the moment each day. Imagine you get a ping on your phone and you are alerted to some just-in-time feedback from your boss: "Hey, Mike, great report. You incorporated the ideas of your colleagues from the task force and the argument is persuasive. Your writing is concise and helps others move to action." Later in the day you get another ping signifying that you have gotten a summarized report from eight people on what you can do "more of" or "less of" based on yesterday's meeting with the client. You skim it quickly. You see some great ideas you can incorporate into your routine. This kind of technology is available and can be easily tailored to different environments.

This approach comes with its own set of challenges and a need for practice in dialogue, coaching conversations, and giving and receiving feedback. This "coaching to performance" approach is beneficial in the following ways:

- dialogue focused, not paper focused
- challenging and supportive, not labeling
- time relevant, not quarterly or full-year snapshots
- behavioral, not vague and general statements
- informs compensation decision later on in the year, but not directly linked to vague compensation constraints.

The cornerstone of such a system is that managers, employees, and the entire organization must learn and adopt a coaching mindset with inherent coaching techniques: powerful dialogue, two-way communication, continuous improvement, concrete development actions that are tracked frequently, and "feed forward agreements" in between coaching meetings. So why does this transform the entire culture? David Rock and colleagues explain that the anxiety that a performance management system (especially rating systems) causes evokes the "fight or flight" response and "is ill-suited for the kind of thoughtful, reflective conversations that allow people to learn from a performance review" (Rock, Davis, and Jones 2014, 3). Thus, they recommend a system that evokes the positive, receptive parts of the brain and emphasizes growth and future possibilities, not the inherent dead-end, nongrowth, fixed mindset of traditional appraisals. They state that fixed mindsets hold people and organizations back because of mental paralysis:

> Conventional performance management has been linked to high levels of attrition, low productivity, and significant problems with collaboration. . . . Evaluations must be based on a growth mindset; they must recognize that with the right context and conditions, anyone's ability can be improved, especially given the expansive, flexible nature of the human brain (Rock, Davis, and Jones 2014, 4).

This is a powerful example of how one pervasive tool can provide not just a behavioral hook, but also a person-to-person immersion into an entire coaching culture.

Measuring and Tracking Results

Remember when all that was used to measure training was the end-of-course "smile" instrument? It is good to know that you now have the right tools and technology to track and measure more meaningful and realistic data;

specifically, data that indicate significant change and impact. What proof do we have that putting money into this coaching program is worth the trouble? What statistics do we have to indicate that a coaching culture produces higher bottom-line results and successful on-the-job behaviors?

The most prevalent tool to measure coaching results is a 360-degree feedback instrument, given before and after a coaching cycle (Sherpa Coaching 2016). This is an important indicator. As we saw in chapter 4, there are a variety of such instruments, some readily available online and some requiring certification. There is also a choice in tools for individual or group and team results. Yet, as coaching has evolved, organizations are asking for indicators of financial benefits and overall organizational impact.

It is wise to use a combination of direct and indirect measures and qualitative and quantitative measures. Using a combination of approaches at multiple levels is usually referred to as measuring return on effectiveness. The best way to ascertain the measures that are most important to your organization—that fit your business and leadership mindset—is to ask. Form focus groups and conduct interviews to brainstorm and finalize a list of measures that will most likely be embraced in your organizational setting. At the same time, gather ideas on the best way to collect such data: Add coaching-specific questions to existing organizational surveys, collect end-of-coaching surveys and 360-degree results, conduct interviews to dig deeper and discover financial impact, work with accounting or finance to identify and collect all costs associated with coaching, and design coaching reports that grab strategic decision makers.

Two of the more sophisticated measures for coaching results are return on investment and impact on business. They rely on gathering information from leadership, management, and employees on what measures are most meaningful; designing a multimethod strategy for collecting that information; and using qualitative and quantitative methodology to collate and report the data. Using such methods, executive coaching has shown to provide return on investment of three to six times cost (Hawkins 2008). Although more work intensive, becoming politically savvy in offering such analytics is becoming paramount in today's world. You need to move beyond the basic results of participant reaction and learning, and measure actual on-the-job application and impact on the entire organization (Kirkpatrick 2006). Organizations are developing separate departments dedicated to organizational analytics. Join forces with such groups, use a consultant, or educate yourself in analytics.

One of the more useful resources for stepping into the world of coaching measures is *Measuring the Success of Coaching* (Phillips, Phillips, and Edwards 2012). Jack and Patricia Phillips provide research, specific formulas, extensive cases and examples, and sample processes for not only obtaining measures, but also making decisions for continuous improvement of the entire coaching process. And that's the main point: Don't just measure; do something with those measures and track improvement based on those changes. They emphasize a multidimensional approach because many factors need to be considered when measuring tangible and intangible benefits and results.

With intangible results (such as level of increased job satisfaction through coaching), more steps are required to transfer the data to monetary form. It is important to ascertain the company's measurement objective at the beginning of collecting data because it will influence how you collect the data, the instrument you use, and the assumptions you are going to apply to the calculations. As you brainstorm the idea of measurement with leaders and groups of employees, it is helpful to create a checklist of what you want to find out from the results: The effectiveness of internal versus external coaches. The relationship between coaching success and coaches who have had more training than others. The costs compared with other learning initiatives. The engagement level before and after another new phase of coaching is added into the culture.

More specifically, if you merely want to discover whether an individual applies certain identified behaviors after a six-month coaching process (measuring application), that can be measured through a pre- and post-360-degree survey. However, if in addition to this you also want to discover the effect that coaching has on raising customer sales or increasing revenue, that will entail additional sets of gathered data and analytical tools (measuring impact). The Phillips recommend planning for collecting data at five levels: satisfaction, learning, application, impact, and ROI (Phillips and Phillips 2005).

Sure, measuring the return on an investment in a person is a bit more difficult than measuring the increase in the number of widgets produced per hour. Tim Morin (2004) provides the following formula, similar to many other such formulas in the literature:

$$\% \text{ ROI} = \text{Benefits Achieved} - \text{Coaching Costs} \times 100$$

Coaching Costs

The challenge is clearly identifying the benefits achieved through the coaching program and assigning a monetary value to those benefits. This is where brainstorming with your company professionals and experts comes in. If they have a say in what goes into such a calculation, they will more readily believe the results. Morin outlines the following steps:

1. Identify what you want to measure and collect baseline measures—even if you and your colleagues (with input from others) need to make experienced assumptions.

2. Measure results using pertinent data-gathering tools and existing documents. Some results are more tangible than others and are easier to translate into monetary value or bottom-line impact. But as Morin points out, "This is not to say that the tangible outweighs the intangible in terms of importance. In fact, intangible changes in the client's behavior can often have a wider-ranging impact than, or may lead to, the more tangible benefits of coaching."

3. Through analytics and formulas, convert benefits into dollars. It is important to be clear and transparent in showing which measures are direct (totally dependent on coaching) versus those correlated to coaching (with coaching being the new or important ingredient), but possibly based on other factors as well. Although it is evident that executive coaching can have a considerable influence on business results, other factors obviously have an impact. Morin (2004) gives this example:

> Say, sales volume is subject to many complex factors, only one of which is coaching (others include economic conditions, product developments, competition, pricing, customer demand, and currency fluctuations). To the extent that you have confidence that the coaching influenced sales volume to some extent, you can apply a percentage adjustment or weighting to the monetary value of the sales increase to reflect this impact. For example,

> if you believe that 25 percent of a $1 million increase in
> sales can be attributed to behavior change prompted by
> the coaching, we would add $250,000 to your "Benefits
> Achieved" number in the formula. This adjustment allows
> us to isolate the effects of the coaching.

Today's business environment requires HR and talent development professionals to provide a return on investment for coaching. The initial setup of tools and measures will be challenging, but once in place, the data will provide important metrics to guide decision making, adjustments, continuous improvement mindsets, and accomplishment of both personal and organization goals: in short, the "stuff" of what makes coaching organizations.

Making It Real

Because coaching programs have become a significant part of organizations, the demand for measures and successful returns has increased. Measuring the impact of coaching both qualitatively and quantitatively must be part of every coach's tool kit. Utilizing a combination of factors and multiple levels of data, you can gather insights into behavioral and bottom-line results. And most important, data keep proving tangible results in many areas: productivity, sales, engagement, morale, confidence, cooperation, and decision making.

This chapter emphasized the absolute necessity of using a systems approach in implementing and hardwiring coaching behaviors into an organization. For coaching to become a habit, the organization must reinforce coaching in all major practices and processes—performance appraisals, meetings protocol, webinars, virtual team coaching sessions, training in coaching techniques, leadership role models, and strategic initiatives. Using concepts from emotional intelligence and neuroscience research further enriches and increases the implementation and growth of coaching cultures.

1. Describe the present performance appraisal process in your organization. What is the typical approach, process, paperwork, mindset, and outcomes? Provide an example of the language typically used.

   - Present performance appraisal scenario:

   - Present language:

2. Based on what you read in this chapter, develop a goal for how the organization can move toward (or improve) a coaching performance appraisal process. Then indicate new language that could be used in the process.
   - Goal:

   - New language:

3. Describe what measures and measurement processes are presently being used in your organization to assess the outcomes of existing coaching efforts.

4. Develop a goal for the type of measures and measurement process that would be more effective in your organization, indicate at least three tools that would be needed, and state the new improved outcomes.
   - Goal:

   - Tools:

   - Outcomes:

8

Looking to the Future

Moving forward, more organizations will likely want to create coaching cultures. There is an energy in those organizations that is palpable and inviting. These are organizations where people "see" one another and individuals know they matter. Learning and practicing the necessary skill sets of dialogue, openness, perspective taking, accountability, mutual support, and continuous improvement—whether in a brick and mortar or virtual organization—is the price of entry, and once admitted, most individuals embrace the opportunities provided. People want to take part, experience the interesting, be heard, feel acknowledged and supported, and grow and contribute. This is a human need. And it is met in coaching organizations.

So, what are the benefits of a coaching organization? In "The Benefits of a Coaching Culture," the author presents research showing that "coaching increases performance, productivity and job satisfaction at all levels" (Yu 2007). In the study, a multinational manufacturer put its managers through a coaching workshop and then surveyed its salespeople three months later to see what results were produced: "The salespeople who reported more intense coaching from their managers also reported a 36% increase in performance."

In another study, Xerox studied the impact of coaching when provided as a follow-up to training and found an 87 percent increase in effectiveness for the participants who received coaching versus those who did not (Auerbach 2005). Finally, Jeffrey Auerbach (2005) cites the following benefits attributed to coaching and reported by participants in a study of Fortune 1000 companies:

- increase in productivity: 53 percent
- increase in customer service: 39 percent

- increased retention of senior people: 32 percent
- increased bottom-line profitability: 22 percent
- reduction in costs: 22 percent.

In the 2014 research paper *Building a Coaching Culture,* the International Coach Federation and the Human Capital Institute conclude, "A robust coaching culture has been linked to higher employee engagement: 65% of employees are highly engaged in strong coaching culture organizations compared to 52% of employees in other organizations. Organizations with a strong coaching culture also report greater financial performance: 60% report being above their industry peer group in 2013 revenue compared to 41% of all others" (HCI and ICF 2014, 28).

The future of coaching cultures is distinct from the future of the field of coaching as a whole, but they certainly influence each other. Coaching organizations—or an individual coaching program—are designed to be in sync with the overall goals of the working environment. If an organization implements a coaching program in which leaders and employees can take part in formal coaching, trains everyone to use dialogue in conversations and meetings, uses a coaching style of performance management, and highlights strategic goals to which coaching skill sets and results are linked, the benefits cascade throughout the enterprise. More studies in this area to link specific causal variables with the outcomes we are describing will undoubtedly be forthcoming.

This phenomenon can also be demonstrated in related fields. For example, the training of leaders in emotional intelligence has proven to raise not only the level of success for individual leaders, but also the bottom-line results of their companies. This is totally understandable when you look at the component skill sets of EI (Bharwaney, Bar-On, and MacKinlay 2011):

- **self-awareness:** realizing your own emotions and drives, knowing how they affect your daily work, and using new skills to manage those emotions in a productive way
- **self-regulation:** suspending judgment and redirecting your disruptive impulses
- **motivation:** pursuing goals with energy and passion beyond money or status
- **empathy:** understanding, connecting, and factoring in the emotions of others when interacting with them
- **social skills:** managing relationships and building networks.

Sound familiar? The elements of EI further support the kind of dialogue, interpersonal strength, human understanding, and new pathways in the brain that distinguish a coaching organization.

Another driving phenomenon is the Millennial generation, who describe traditional companies as places that "suck out your soul." What do they want so they can do their best? Again, it sounds like a prescription for a coaching organization (Impraise 2016). According to Impraise, Millennials want someone to:

- Help them navigate their career.
- Give them straight feedback.
- Mentor and coach them.
- Sponsor them for formal development programs.
- Provide flexible schedules.
- Listen to them and acknowledge their thoughts, and explain the "why" and "why not" in a supportive, not dismissive way.
- Provide opportunities for social impact.

The research cited in this book supports the fact that these needs are human needs, no matter how old you are! Going beyond Millennials, a coaching environment supports the needs of all generations by:

- engaging workers of all ages
- engaging and sparking interest
- fostering positive working relationships and actions
- increasing individual productivity
- raising the bottom line.

So why don't more organizations choose to create coaching cultures? As stated in chapter 1, the vision and mission of some organizations is to mindfully ignore the employees and align everyone in the pursuit of making money. At different times in people's lives, this may be the kind of driver they might want to pursue until other needs force them to recalibrate their priorities. Another reason is inertia. A company may be profitable, so why change? Sure, there might be turnover, but essentially the company is on solid ground and issues seem to right themselves when they get too far off track. This inertia is another characteristic within human nature, in which people and entire enterprises ignore something until it gets bad enough to do something about.

When you commit to coaching throughout an organization, you are unleashing the talent of each person and the organization as a whole. To do so, create your vision, assess the organization's readiness, and then purposefully begin making coaching a part of your organization's DNA. The work takes time (sometimes several years), an investment in resources and energy, and strong leadership to establish a coaching culture. Revisit the Phillips Corporation case study in chapter 7. Presently, the people leaders at Phillips are continuing to develop new ways to capture the "growth brains" of the employees and generate passion in them. They are relentless in this task. Their vision is very clear: virtuosos engaging in dialogue to create the better idea. At Phillips, dialogue leads to powerful conversation. As Theodore Zeldin explains, "Conversation is a meeting of minds with different memories and habits. When minds meet, they don't just exchange facts: they transform them, reshape them, draw different implications from them, engage in new trains of thought. Conversation doesn't just reshuffle the cards: it creates new cards" (Krznaric 2014). The result? A profitable machine-tool company with a dynamic coaching culture that has survived several economic downturns and has expanded into China and India.

As a leader or practitioner trying to build a coaching culture, you need to be ready for certain people who will decide to leave the organization because they can't or won't adapt to a coaching environment. That's OK. They need to move on to places where they can work more comfortably. Remember, coaching is about making choices—and choices lead to change.

Coaching Trends and Opportunities

A review of trends in the field of coaching informs actions to be leveraged when building coaching organizations. Coaching has found its place in the mainstream and is here to stay. So, how can we build on the foundation that has been created? As with any maturing field, it is important to take stock and address obstacles and opportunities. As early as 2003, executive coaches Sheila Maher and Suzi Pomerantz stressed the importance of continually assessing the coaching field and taking action to remain relevant, leading edge, and of value to clients.

From combing much research for this book, and from our own 20-plus years in the field, we see the following trends that practitioners need to watch and influence:

The Economy

Coaching declined during the last recession and then surged when the economy slowly recovered. During the downturn, organizations restructured to do more with less. The results after the recovery are interesting. Organizations did not return to what they were before the recession. Rather, they stayed leaner and more mindful of the type of employees needed for the future. In this new environment, coaching became a strategic way to develop and engage people for the newly defined future. Coaching is being used to build corporate brands, hire the right employees, and ensure continuous development.

Implication and opportunity: Coaching will continue to grow and be a recognized component for organizational health and success. More and more organizations will utilize internal and external coaches serving all employees throughout the enterprise to support their coaching cultures.

Millennials and Different Generations

There are more than 53 million Millennials in today's workforce, making them the single largest age cohort in decades (Fry 2015). Millennials want frequent feedback, ongoing growth discussions, and open-minded dialogue. And guess what? So do members of every generation.

Implication and opportunity: Coaching cultures provide the kind of environment that will attract, develop, and retain the best and brightest of not only Millennials, but any generation.

Analytics and Bottom-Line Results

Analytics are in demand in every industry to prove results and make decisions. While many individuals and organizations are looking for a clear, causal link between coaching and ROI, practitioners and researchers such as Anthony Grant (2012) have proposed a more robust measure of coaching impact: WBEF, the well-being and engagement framework. Whatever measures are utilized, coaching practitioners need to become educated in and partner with those who have measurement expertise. Analytical results prove the value of coaching for both behavioral and bottom-line results. Gathering such data—including when organizations do so in formulating measurement criteria—and publicizing reliable results will support the future of coaching organizations.

Implication and opportunity: The most successful coaches will be those who understand, use, and encourage the use of measures to support coaching infrastructures. Organizations that track coaching results using both tangible and intangible factors will have more sustainable success. Publicizing such results in the literature will further coaching credibility and professionalism.

Credentialing, Research, and Marketing

There are many definitions of coaching in the field, often propagated by different gurus, authors, researchers, and accreditation bodies trying to claim their corner of the market. This is troubling in terms of consistency, professionalism, and alignment of expertise and qualifications across practitioners. Because there is money to be made through credentialing, the proliferation of different avenues is understandable but sensitive There are many coaching niches ("life coach," "wellness coach," "spiritual coach") and a wide range of pay scales, approaches, and results. These circumstances are causing market saturation and watering down the skills needed to be an effective coach.

Implication and opportunity: It is important—for the integrity and credibility of the coaching profession—that those in the coaching field work together in codifying and aligning what is required in terms of standards, ethics, certification, and credentialing expertise. Similar to credentialing in medicine, law, and accounting, there should be a limited number of qualifying bodies with clear and consistent approaches to ensure credibility. This, in turn, would streamline research studies and analytics so the field can have greater impact. By working together, different entities can agree on the right balance of regulation and flexibility. Such cooperation and consistent messaging can foster reliability and respect.

Relationships

Connecting effectively with others is a growing challenge. Most individuals in 2017 spend more time on their various devices and social media than they do in face-to-face communication. More access and less awareness contribute to weaker connections. A large percentage of communication at work is electronic, and many people will text or email each other rather than call or seek out an in-person meeting, even when they are co-located. The preponderance of reality stars and technology has created an environment where we may know more about complete strangers than we do our colleagues.

Implication and opportunity: As Kim Scott tells leaders, "Your relationships are core to your job and you have to build relationships of trust. . . .

Only when you actually care about the whole person with your whole self can you build a relationship" (2017, xvii, 13). There is a tremendous opportunity to connect with others and build a vibrant network that will support discovery and learning. This is the heart of a coaching organization.

Technology

Technology has infiltrated every part of our lives. Leveraging technology is important for coaching to remain accessible and relevant. This can include the use of mobile applications, webinars, video, and software tools.

Implication and opportunity: To ensure that coaching can be used under different circumstances and time constraints—whether face-to-face or virtual—it is necessary to embrace technology. In her 2016 whitepaper, Carol Goldsmith describes three kinds of coaches: "high-tech, low-tech, and no-tech" (27). Coaches and coaching cultures need to creatively use feedback tools, data-gathering software, web-based learning, mobile apps, and other technology-driven support structures to enhance coaching delivery and effectiveness. We need to be leaders in partnering with technology to ensure this support platform.

Coach and coach trainer Julia Stewart (2011) talks about trends and the future of coaching and looks at coaching 10, 20, and 30 years out. She points out that "coaching will no longer be considered exotic or only for the rich and famous. It will be as common as personal training is today. . . . More dramatically, as a result of the growth in coaching, society will evolve, with more people living values-driven lives."

Despite the impact of coaching and multiple survey results linking higher productivity and engagement, strong retention, decreased conflict, and increased customer satisfaction, only 13 percent of the organizations participating in *Building a Coaching Culture With Managers and Leaders* reported a "strong coaching culture" (HCI and ICF 4). Clearly, we have a way to go to make coaching language and culture the organizational norm.

So our work is cut out for us. The future is exciting for coaching and coaching cultures—and even coaching societies. And it's dynamic for those of us who are fortunate enough to live in and work to create coaching cultures. They are truly transformational. While in practice, each organization is characterized by their own unique implementation, coaching cultures share the same heart: high energy, a strong commitment, a belief in the work, a dedication to colleagues and customers, a desire to help, a service mindset, a results focus, and a desire to deliver. This is the kind of environment that most people dream about. But you can make this environment, this dream, a reality for your organization. We wish you luck in so doing.

Making It Real

This concluding chapter emphasized coaching cultures as an important component of your future in the working world. The essence of coaching is what makes human beings feel connected, productive, and engaged. It also enables strategic and bottom-line success.

1. If you were going to start a company from scratch, write a goal that would support the building of a coaching culture.
2. Of the six coaching trends outlined in this chapter, choose one that resonates with you.
   - Describe the state of that trend in terms of present mindset, behaviors, and results.
   - Envision that positive movement has been made on that trend. Describe that future mindset, behaviors, and results.
3. Given what you have learned in this book, write a personal goal for yourself in terms of how you will incorporate the things you want to be doing and saying one year from now.

Appendix

Dialogue in Action

Let's revisit the role play between Paul and John from chapter 1. In it, Paul uses language to create a safe space where John can share his frustrations. Paul demonstrates active listening and powerful questioning to support John in thinking through his frustration. He helps him identify skills that he's used in the past that he might apply in this situation. Notice the rhythm and tone of the conversation. See the inserted notes, highlighting the power of dialogue.

Paul: John, you look frustrated or annoyed, I can't tell which. Are you having problems with the project team? *Establishes coaching context; no negative judgment; positive intent and questioning.*

John: Is it that noticeable? I guess it is written all over my face. I'm both frustrated and annoyed! Yes, the project team is having difficulties, and the real problem is the client. *Hidden, transparent thoughts come to the fore; reasoning explained.*

Paul: How is the client being difficult, and how is that affecting the contract? What's going on? *Further expanding the reasoning and positive intent through questions.*

John: Johnson keeps changing his mind. I have had clients change their minds, and I know how to manage such situations and keep the client happy. What's making this difficult is Johnson keeps blaming me and the team. I've tried using change reports and showing him that everything we are doing is in line with what he shared in the last meeting.

Unfortunately, he comes up with all these "far out" ideas in between the meetings and I'm having trouble managing that behavior. *Further expanding the pool of knowledge because he feels safe.*

Paul: Interesting. You say he doesn't respond positively to change reports or being reminded of what he said before? Can you think of a way to move him forward, not making a big deal about him changing his mind, while still keeping everything within the scope of the project? *Powerful question to get John to see beyond his "stuck" point.*

John: That's my point. That's what I keep trying to do. I'm stuck. *Natural resistance and acknowledges he is stuck and might need help. Is now open to more listening and alternatives.*

Paul: Remember about two years ago—I know it was a while back—you were assisting me with Jane Morgan? She was a real pain, remember? *Creating a future scenario with a similar story. Captures John. Puts John in another place beyond being stuck. Suggests other pathways.*

John: I sure do. I can't believe how you kept your cool from meeting to meeting. Let me see. I remember you stayed positive. You always complimented her on her great ideas. Oh, wow, I remember now; you kept saying, "Oh, I see you have done some additional thinking from the last time we talked." *John begins to see the connections and possibilities. He starts to reframe his situation.*

Paul: That's right. I never demonstrated any frustration. In fact, remember that one time when she did a complete 180 and I said, "Wow, what creative thinking!" I saw you trying to hold in your laughter. *Further learning added to the pool of knowledge.*

John: Yep. And, I get your point. She loved the compliments. *Homing in on the learning.*

Paul: And, quite frankly, her additional ideas and thinking had merit from time to time. So, it was important for me to listen and figure out how her newest idea could be easily done or whether it required an additional adjustment to the contract. *Suggesting alternative reaction to the situation and thus alternative action other than frustration.*

John: Yes, I see what you mean. *Clear acknowledgment from coachee.*

Paul: A question I like to ask myself is, "How can I build a bridge between what the client now wants and what we had previously agreed to?" That tends to put me in a problem-solving frame of mind, and I can take the client along the path with me. *Coach offers a helpful tool and helps coachee see how that can be used in this future scenario they are building.*

John: Yep. That is probably something that will work with Johnson. Coachee has reframed and can see himself trying this out. *Coachee has moved beyond being stuck into choice and declaration.*

Paul: I think it will. What I have found, John—see what you think about this—is that most people just want to be heard. Some clients can get all their thoughts out in one swoop and one neat contract. Others need you to stop and help them catch up at every meeting. How might you incorporate this in your next meeting with Johnson? *Coach makes a specific request now that coachee sees the picture. Coach further expands on the rationale and the consequences of the new behavior. Coach also engages coachee and asks a question to keep coachee on the path with him. Coach is holding coachee's agenda and encourages him to continue to play out the steps and action. This further solidifies that the behavior will be tried and practiced.*

John: As you said, sometimes it just means making a minor adjustment, and other times I might need to say, "I really like that idea and I believe it will make the product stronger. It will mean two more weeks of production that I will need to add to the contract. Is this OK with you, or would you like to rethink how we might go about this?"

Paul: Exactly. That's how I would handle it. Is this helpful? How might you take this and apply it to reduce your frustration and get closer to the result you are seeking? *Getting agreement and establishing accountability.*

John: I'm meeting with Johnson on Friday. I'm definitely going to try it. It should work until the next frustration comes along! Thanks, Paul. *Choice, open declaration of action, and accountability.*

Paul: Sounds good. I'll come by on Monday to find out how it went. Given that I have not worked with Johnson before, maybe you can share some additional tips with me! *Sealing the accountability and re-establishing the trust of mutual learning.*

With Paul's help, John will be moving to greater satisfaction and success. This kind of interaction equates to higher performance for individuals, teams, and organizations, which in turn tends to spread to suppliers, customers, and the community. Learning is contagious.

References

Anderson, D. 2015. *Organization Development: The Process of Leading Organizational Change,* 3rd ed. Thousand Oaks, CA: Sage.

Arbinger Institute. 2016. *The Outward Mindset: Seeing Beyond Ourselves.* Oakland, CA: Berrett-Koehler.

Argyris, C. 1977. "Double Loop Learning in Organizations." *Harvard Business Review,* September. https://hbr.org/1977/09/double-loop-learning-in -organizations.

Auerbach, J.E. 2005. "The Benefits of Business Coaching." College of Executive Coaching. www.executivecoachcollege.com/research-and-publications/benefits -of-business-coaching.php.

Beckhard, R. 1969. *Organization Development: Strategies and Models.* Reading, MA: Addison-Wesley.

Belf, T., and G. Meli. 2011. "Increasing Personal and Professional Effectiveness." An Introduction to Coaching training course. Reston, VA: Success Unlimited Network.

Bharwaney, G., R. Bar-On, and A. MacKinlay. 2011. *EQ and the Bottom Line: Emotional Intelligence Increases Individual Occupational Performance, Leadership and Organisational Productivity.* Bedfordshire, UK: Ei World Limited, 1-39. www.eiconsortium.org/pdf/Bharwaney_BarOn_MacKinlay _EQ_and_Bottom_Line.pdf.

Bianco-Mathis, V. 2016. "Train Your Brain." Expertise + Experience, Marymount's HRM blog, August 10. http://learn.marymount.edu/hrmblog/train-your-brain.

Bianco-Mathis, V., and L. Nabors. 2015. "Tools." The Dialogue Deck. http:// dialoguedeck.com/tools.

Bianco-Mathis, V., L. Nabors, and C. Roman. 2002. *Leading From the Inside Out: A Coaching Model.* Thousand Oaks, CA: Sage.

Bianco-Mathis, V., C. Roman, and L. Nabors. 2008. *Organizational Coaching: Building Relationships and Strategies That Drive Results.* Alexandria, VA: ASTD Press.

Buckingham, M., and A. Goodall. 2015. "Reinventing Performance Management." *Harvard Business Review,* April. https://hbr.org/2015/04/reinventing -performance-management.

Coutu, D., and C. Kauffman. 2009. "What Can Coaches Do for You?" *Harvard Business Review,* January. https://hbr.org/2009/01/what-can-coaches-do-for-you.

Doran, G. 1981. "There's a Smart Way to Write Management Goals and Objectives: S. M. A. R. T." *Management Review* 70(11): 35-36.

Falconer, L. 2017. "5 Powerful Reasons Why Goal Setting Is Important." Code of Living, April 26. www.codeofliving.com/life/goals/5-powerful-reasons-why-goal-setting-is-important.

Fry, R. 2015. "Millennials Surpass Gen Xers as the Largest Generation in U.S. Labor Force." Pew Research Center, March 11. www.pewresearch.org/fact-tank/2015/05/11/millennials-surpass-gen-xers-as-the-largest-generation-in-u-s-labor-force.

Goleman, D. 1998. *Working With Emotional Intelligence.* New York: Bantam Books.

———. 2000. "Leadership That Gets Results." *Harvard Business Review,* March. https://hbr.org/2000/03/leadership-that-gets-results.

Goldsmith, C. 2016. *Ten Trends Driving Organizational Coaching.* Library of Professional Coaching, December 21. http://libraryofprofessionalcoaching.com/concepts/strategy/future-of-coaching/ten-trends-driving-organizational-coaching.

Goodman, R. 2002. "Coaching Senior Executives for Effective Business Leadership." In *Executive Coaching,* edited by C. Fitzgerald and J. Berger, 135-153. Palo Alto, CA: Davies-Black.

Goss, T. 1996. *The Last Word on Power.* New York: Doubleday.

Grant, A.M. 2012. "ROI Is a Poor Measure of Coaching Success: Towards a More Holistic Approach Using a Well-Being and Engagement Framework." *Coaching* 1(12). www.coachfederation.org/files/includes/docs/156-ROI-is-a-Poor-Measure-of-Coaching-Success--2012.pdf.

Hargrove, R. 1995. *Masterful Coaching: Extraordinary Results by Impacting People and the Way They Think and Work Together.* San Francisco: Jossey-Bass.

Hawkins, R. 2008. *Measuring the ROI of Coaching.* Coatesville, PA: Take Charge Consultants. http://takechargeinc.com/wp-content/uploads/2011/01/Measuring-the-ROI-on-coaching3.pdf.

HCI (Human Capital Institute) and ICF (International Coach Federation). 2014. *Building a Coaching Culture.* Cincinnati: Human Capital Institute.

———. 2016. *Building a Coaching Culture With Managers and Leaders.* Cincinnati: Human Capital Institute.

ICF (International Coach Federation). 2016. *2016 Global Coaching Study, Executive Summary.* Lexington, KY: ICF. www.coachfederation.org/about /landing.cfm?ItemNumber=3936.

Impraise. 2016. *The Benefits of Real-Time Feedback.* New York: Impraise. www.impraise.com/resources/#white-papers.

Isaacs, W. 1999. *Dialogue: The Art of Thinking Together.* New York: Random House.

Kirkpatrick, D. 2006. *Evaluating Training Programs: The Four Levels,* 3rd ed. San Francisco: Berrett-Koehler.

Krznaric, R. 2014. *Empathy: Why It Matters, and How to Get It.* New York: Penguin.

Lipman, V. 2014. "New Study Answers: What Motivates Employees to 'Go the Extra Mile'?" *Forbes,* November 4. www.forbes.com/sites/victorlipman /2014/11/04/what-motivates-employees-to-go-the-extra-mile -study-offers-surprising-answer/#.

Maher, S., and S. Pomerantz. 2003. "The Future of Executive Coaching: Analysis From a Market Life Cycle Approach." *International Journal of Coaching* 1(2): 3-11.

Matthews, J. 2010. "Can Line Managers Ever Be Effective Coaches?" *Business Leadership Review* VII(II): 1-10.

Morin, Tim. 2004. "Calculating ROI From Executive Coaching." WJM Associates: News, Advice & Insight, October. www.wjmassoc.com/insight/roi-executive -coaching-on-boarding.

Parker, I. 2015. *Handbook of Critical Psychology.* New York: Routledge.

Parsloe, E., and M. Leedham. 2016. *Coaching and Mentoring: Practical Techniques for Developing Learning and Performance.* London: Kogan Press.

Passmore, J., and A. Fillery-Travis. 2011. "A Critical Review of Executive Coaching Research: A Decade of Progress and What's to Come." *Coaching: An International Journal of Theory, Research and Practice* 4(2): 70-88.

Phillips, J.J., and P.P. Phillips. 2005. "Measuring ROI in Executive Coaching." *International Journal of Coaching in Organizations* 3(1): 53-62.

Phillips, P.P., J.J. Phillips, and L. Edwards. 2012. *Measuring the Success of Coaching.* Alexandria, VA: ASTD Press.

Rock, D. 2006. *Quiet Leadership: Six Steps to Transforming Performance at Work.* New York: HarperCollins.

———. 2009. "Managing With the Brain in Mind." *strategy + business,* August 27. www.strategy-business.com/article/09306?gko=5df7f.

———. 2013. "Learning About the Brain Changes Everything." Posted by TEDx, February 1. www.youtube.com/watch?v=uDIyxxayNig.

Rock, D., J. Davis, and E. Jones. 2014. "Kill Your Performance Ratings." *strategy + business,* August 8. www.strategy-business.com/article/00275?gko=c442b.

Rock, D., and L. Page. 2009. *Coaching With the Brain in Mind: Foundations for Practice.* Hoboken, NJ: John Wiley & Sons.

Scott, K. 2017. *Radical Candor: How to Be a Kick-Ass Boss Without Losing Your Humanity.* New York: St. Martin's Press.

Senge, P. 1990. *The Fifth Discipline: The Art and Practice of Learning Organizations.* New York: Doubleday.

Sherpa Coaching. 2016. *Sherpa 2016 Executive Coaching Study.* Cincinnati: Sherpa Coaching. www.sherpacoaching.com/annual-executive-coaching-survey.

———. 2017. *Corporate Culture Survey.* Cincinnati: Sherpa Coaching. http://sherpacoaching.com/pdf%20files/2016_Corporate_Culture_Report_Sherpa _Coaching.pdf.

Shook, E. 2015. "Dump Performance Appraisals . . . and Help Employees Be Their Best." *Huffington Post,* August 4. www.huffingtonpost.com/ellyn-shook /dump-performance-appraisals-and-help-employees-be-their-best_b_7933268 .html.

Sieler, A. 2016. "The Conversational Nature of Leadership and Management." *Newfield Institute,* February 12. www.talkingabout.com.au/sites/default/files /TheConversationalNatureofLeadership.pdf.

Staub, R.E. 1996. *The Heart of Leadership.* Provo, UT: Executive Excellence Publishing.

Stewart, J. 2011. "Coaching Trends and the Future of Coaching." Coaching Blog. www.schoolofcoachingmastery.com/coaching-blog/bid/55009/Coaching -Trends-the-Future-of-Coaching.

Stober, D., and A. Grant, eds. 2006. *Evidence-Based Coaching Handbook: Putting Best Practices to Work for Your Clients.* Hoboken, NJ: John Wiley & Sons.

Stone, D., and S. Heen. 2014. *Thanks for the Feedback: The Science and Art of Receiving Feedback Well.* New York: Penguin.

Whitmore, J. 2011. *Coaching for Performance,* 4th ed. Boston: Nicholas Brealey Publishers.

Yu, L. 2007. "The Benefits of a Coaching Culture." MIT Sloan Management Review, January 1. http://sloanreview.mit.edu/article/the-benefits-of-a -coaching-culture.

About the Authors

 **Virginia Bianco-Mathis** is a professor and chairperson at Marymount University School of Business Administration, and co-founder and partner of Strategic Performance Group. She earned a master's degree from Johns Hopkins and a doctorate in human and organization development from George Washington University. She has held leadership positions with companies in the aerospace, financial real estate, and telecommunications fields.

Virginia possesses expertise in strategy, organization change, performance management, leadership, and executive coaching. Her passion is identifying issues and opportunities through organizational diagnosis and assisting leaders in moving their organizations through the implementation of change and attainment of bottom-line success. She has been labeled a "silver bullet," being able to zero in on the exact combination of factors needed to achieve an envisioned future. Her practical, direct approach is based on dialogue, observable behaviors, and building infrastructures to support measurable results.

Presently, Virginia is involved in major projects with Haystax Technology, Seyfarth Shaw, and Fannie Mae. She sits on the Board of Phillips Corporation and has published widely in the fields of coaching, team development, and leadership. In particular, she guest lectures for Leadership Arlington in Northern Virginia, writes a monthly blog (http://learn.marymount.edu/hrmblog), and delivers worldwide presentations. Having co-authored several international books and courses on coaching, including The Dialogue Deck, she encourages leaders to paint a picture and consider the consequences of doing nothing. She lives in Annandale, Virginia, with her husband and three children, who tend to move in and out of the main homestead.

Lisa Nabors is a co-founder and partner of Strategic Performance Group and is recognized by the International Coach Federation as a professional certified coach. Lisa is a sought-after speaker and keynote, presenting on the topic of coaching to industry and professional groups. She began coaching while pursuing a 16-year stint as a senior-level human resource and training and development professional in private industry. Her passion is in optimizing individual, team, and organization performance across a diverse spectrum of professional environments. Her coaching clients include managers, executives, and teams in organizations such as AARP, American Institute of Architects, Council of Better Business Bureaus, Public Interest Registry, and the U.S. Department of Agriculture. Lisa's expertise includes gathering and optimizing data to cut to the core issues, help clients consider choices, and create action plans designed to achieve specific, measurable results.

Nabors is a certified user of all Center for Creative Leadership 360-degree feedback instruments, the EQ-i 2.0 and EQ 360, Leadership Practices Inventory, the Team Emotional Social Intelligence Survey, the Myers-Briggs Type Indicator, FIRO-B, and many other customized instruments. She earned bachelor of arts and master of education degrees from the University of Maryland, where she also completed doctoral-level coursework on leadership effectiveness.

In 2007, Lisa served as subject matter expert and editor for the Association for Talent Development Coaching Certificate Program and co-authored its redesign in 2013. She has facilitated the program nationally and internationally and helped create the online version. She is an adjunct faculty member for Marymount University and the co-author of The Dialogue Deck, *Leading From the Inside Out: A Coaching Model,* and *Organizational Coaching: Building Relationships and Programs That Drive Results.* Lisa is passionate about removing but, although, and however from conversation and communicating directly with care. She lives in Herndon, Virginia, with her husband; her pit bull terrier, Dillon; and an ever-expanding garden and blackberry patch.

Index

In this index, *f* denotes figure and *t* denotes table.

fit, 60–61
focus groups, 74
focusing, 39–41, 39t, 47t
future
    of coaching, 136–140
    of coaching culture, 134–135

G

goals and measures, 96–99, 97–98t
Goldsmith, Carol, 139
Goleman, Daniel, 16, 19, 121
Goodman, Robert, 20
Goss, Tracy, 20
Grant, Anthony, 137
group observation, 75

H

Hargrove, Robert, 3
health management programs, 116–117
Heen, Sheila, 72
Heidegger, Martin, 20
homogenized raw data, 77–78
Human Capital Institute, 134, 139
hypothesis statements, 78

I

ICF (International Coach Federation), 4,
    134, 139
image studies, 74
impact on business, 128–129
impatience, 104
Impraise, 135
inconsistency in data, 77
individual and group observation, 75
inference, ladder of, 35–38
internal challenges, 103. See also resistance
internal colleagues, 73
International Coach Federation (ICF), 4,
    134, 139
interpretation, 35–38
Isaacs, William, 35

J

journaling, 99

L

labels, 83
ladder of inference, 35–38
language, positive, 98
Last Word on Power, The (Goss), 20
law firm pilot coaching program, 1–2
"Learning About the Brain Changes Every-
    thing" (Rock), 121
listening, 39t, 41–42, 47t

M

Maher, Sheila, 136
management by objectives, 96–97
marketing, 138
Masterful Coaching (Hargrove), 3
Measuring the Success of Coaching (Phil-
    lips, Phillips, and Edwards), 129
Meli, Giuseppe, 97
mental models, 5–6, 7t
mentoring, 23t
Millennials, 135, 137
mindmap action plans, 95f. See also
    Construct a Plan (Seven Cs Coaching
    Map)
mindset, 67, 79–80
moment, coaching in the, 14
Morin, Tim, 129–131
motivation, 134

N

negotiation
    as dialogue building block, 39t, 45–46,
        48t
    skills improvement, 28–32
neuroscience, 121–122
novelty effect, 121

O

Objectives (C-O-A-CH model), 30, 31t
observation
    as data source, 65t, 66–67
    direct, 65t, 66–67, 106–107, 106t
    feedback from, 106–107, 106t
    individual and group, 75
observers, 106–107, 106t
one-on-one feedback, 75